HUMAN RIGHTS

A N D

THE POLITICS OF TERROR

IDEAS in CONFLICT
Gary E. McCuen

publications inc.

411 Mallalieu Drive
Hudson, Wisconsin 54016
Phone (715) 386-7113

Illustration and Photo Credits

Amnesty International 22; Tony Auth 101, 140; Carol & Simpson 11, 79, 107, 128; Joe Heller 37; Dick Locher 170; Jeff MacNelly 17; Pat Oliphant 70, 162; Mike Ramirez 64; Steve Sack 176; David Seavey 44; John Trever 153; Richard Wright 55, 95, 158, 181

© 1995 by Gary E. McCuen Publications, Inc.
411 Mallalieu Drive, Hudson, Wisconsin 54016

(715) 386-7113

International Standard Book Number
ISBN 0-86596-098-4
Printed in the United States of America

CONTENTS

Chapter 3 THE POLITICS OF TERROR

Chapter 4 HUMANITARIAN INTERVENTION

IDEAS
in CONFLICT

This series features ideas in conflict on political, social, and moral issues. It presents counterpoints, debates, opinions, commentary, and analysis for use in libraries and classrooms. Each title in the series uses one or more of the following basic elements:

Introductions *that present an issue overview giving historic background and/or a description of the controversy.*

Counterpoints *and debates carefully chosen from publications, books, and position papers on the political right and left to help librarians and teachers respond to requests that treatment of public issues be fair and balanced.*

Symposiums *and forums that go beyond debates that can polarize and oversimplify. These present commentary from across the political spectrum that reflect how complex issues attract many shades of opinion.*

A *global* *emphasis with foreign perspectives and surveys on various moral questions and political issues that will help readers to place subject matter in a less culture-bound and ethnocentric frame of reference. In an ever-shrinking and interdependent world, understanding and cooperation are essential. Many issues are global in nature and can be effectively dealt with only by common efforts and international understanding.*

Reasoning skill *study guides and discussion activities provide ready-made tools for helping with critical reading and evaluation of content. The guides and activities deal with one or more of the following:*

RECOGNIZING AUTHOR'S POINT OF VIEW

INTERPRETING EDITORIAL CARTOONS

VALUES IN CONFLICT

WHAT IS EDITORIAL BIAS?

WHAT IS SEX BIAS?

WHAT IS POLITICAL BIAS?

WHAT IS ETHNOCENTRIC BIAS?

WHAT IS RACE BIAS?

WHAT IS RELIGIOUS BIAS?

From across **the political spectrum** *varied sources are presented for research projects and classroom discussions. Diverse opinions in the series come from magazines, newspapers, syndicated columnists, books, political speeches, foreign nations, and position papers by corporations and nonprofit institutions.*

About the Editor

Gary E. McCuen is an editor and publisher of anthologies for public libraries and curriculum materials for schools. Over the past years his publications have specialized in social, moral and political conflict. They include books, pamphlets, cassettes, tabloids, filmstrips and simulation games, many of them designed from his curriculums during 11 years of teaching junior and senior high school social studies. At present he is the editor and publisher of the *Ideas in Conflict* series.

CHAPTER 1

HUMAN RIGHTS: AN OVERVIEW

1

HUMAN RIGHTS: AN OVERVIEW

TORTURE, DETENTION AND HUMAN RIGHTS

John Shattuck

John Shattuck wrote the following article as Assistant Secretary of State for Human Rights and Humanitarian Affairs in the Clinton Administration. This article was an introduction to the Country Reports on Human Rights Practices. The Report is issued every year by the United States Department of State. The reports cover the human rights practices of all nations that are members of the United Nations and a few that are not. They are printed to assist members of Congress in the consideration of legislation, particularly foreign assistance legislation.

Points to Consider:

1. Describe the nature and extent of armed conflict in the world.

2. Summarize the nature of human rights violations.

3. What nations are mentioned as human rights violators?

4. How are global violations of women's rights and worker's rights described?

John Shattuck, "Country Reports on Human Rights Practices," U.S. Department of State, February, 1994.

9

The practice of forced labor continues, as does the abuse of expatriate workers, particularly domestics. Slavery still exists in some countries, particularly in Mauritania and Sudan.

In Bosnia, Sudan, Burundi, Somalia, Angola, Iraq, Azerbaijan, Georgia, and elsewhere, armed conflict led to massive numbers of civilian deaths, refugee flows, and human rights abuses. Many of the conflicts were stimulated by irresponsible political leaders who played on people's fears.

In many parts of the former Yugoslavia, the carnage continues. All nationalities were victimized, and there were numerous violations of the Geneva Conventions. Bosnian Serb armed forces, supported by Belgrade and by Serbian paramilitary counterparts, persisted in their program of "ethnic cleansing," including laying siege to cities, indiscriminately shelling civilian inhabitants, raping and executing noncombatants, and interfering with humanitarian aid deliveries. The warfare continued relentlessly through 1993, with Bosnian government and Croat forces also committing egregious abuses.

• In Sudan, both the Government and the Sudanese People's Liberation Army (SPLA) engaged in widespread human rights abuses, including torture, forced displacement, and massacres of civilians.

• In Somalia, although massive starvation was averted by international humanitarian efforts, most Somalis remained beyond the rule and protection of recognized law and social order.

• In Iraq, Saddam Hussein's regime continued its flagrant abuses of human rights by conducting military operations against civilians, including burning and razing villages, and forcing people to abandon their homes, particularly Shi'a Arabs living in the wetlands of southern Iraq.

• In Azerbaijan, the continuing conflict over Nagorno-Karabakh gave rise to human rights abuses by all sides.

In the Georgian province of Abkhazia, Abkhaz separatists launched a reign of terror after a successful offensive gave them control of the province. Many Georgian civilians and troops were subjected to torture and summary execution.

Cartoon by Carol & Simpson.

TORTURE, ARBITRARY DETENTION, AND THE IMPUNITY OF ABUSERS

Major violations of human rights occurred not only in war-torn countries. Human rights abuses also remained widespread in countries in which violators were not held accountable. When violators can commit human rights abuses with impunity, abuses multiply.

• In Iran, the Government continued to torture and execute people summarily and to restrict the freedoms of speech, press, assembly, and association. Minority religious groups, including the Baha'is, faced systematic repression.

• North Korea remains one of the most repressive countries of the world. The Government treats individual rights as potentially subversive of the goals of the State and the party.

• In Burma, the autocratic military regime reinforces its power with a pervasive security apparatus. People are arrested arbitrarily and prisoners are abused. Citizens are denied basic political rights and the rights of free speech and assembly.

• Zaire is undergoing its worst human rights crisis since the end of the civil war in the 1960s. The Mobutu regime was responsible for massive human rights violations, including extrajudicial killings, unlawful detentions, ethnic violence, torture, and disappearances.

• In China, fundamental human rights provided for in the Chinese Constitution frequently are ignored in practice, and challenges to the Communist Party's political authority are often dealt with harshly and arbitrarily. China took some positive but limited steps in human rights areas, including releasing prominent political prisoners. Hundreds, perhaps thousands, of political prisoners, however, remained under detention or in prison. Reports of physical abuse persisted, including torture by police and prison officials. This was especially the case in politically restive and minority-populated regions such as Tibet.

In Indonesia, extrajudicial arrests and detentions, as well as torture of those in custody, continued. In East Timor, no significant progress was noted in the accounting for those missing from the shooting incident in Dili.

THE RIGHTS OF WOMEN

We have paid special attention to the problem of rampant discrimination against women. Physical abuse is the most obvious example. In many African countries, the practice of female genital mutilation continues. In Pakistan, many women in police custody are subjected to sexual or physical violence. On several continents, women and girls are sold into prostitution. In many Gulf countries, domestic servants from Southeast Asia are forced to work excessively long hours and are sometimes physically and sexually abused. In Bangladesh and India, dowry deaths continue. Marital rape in many countries is not recognized as a crime, and women raped or beaten at home often have no recourse. That female life is not valued as much as male life is apparent in countries such as China where it is reported that more female fetuses than male are aborted.

In addition to physical abuse, the political, civil and legal rights of women are often denied. Women throughout the world are subjected to onerous and discriminatory restrictions of such fundamental freedoms as voting, marriage, travel, testifying in court, inheriting and owning property, and obtaining custody of children. All too often, women and girls find that their access to education, employment, health care, and even food is limited because of their gender.

WORKER RIGHTS

In far too many countries, the freedom of workers to associate, which is the paramount right on which trade unions base their ability to bargain collectively, defend their members' grievances, and protect them from unfair and unsafe working conditions, falls well short of the standards elaborated by the International Labor Organization (ILO). Restrictions on freedom of association abound. They range from outright and total government control of all forms of worker organizations to webs of legislation so complicated that full compliance is virtually impossible, giving authorities excuses to intervene at will.

The practice of forced labor continues, as does the abuse of expatriate workers, particularly domestics. Slavery still exists in some countries, particularly in Mauritania and Sudan. Given the rising concern about the impact of international trade on worker rights standards, this year's reports focus more sharply on the presence of child labor in export industries and on minimum wage and occupational safety standards. Our reports document a number of serious bonded and child labor problems, particularly in South Asia and North Africa.

ACCOUNTABILITY

In the face of widespread human rights violations, the impunity of violators and absence of the rule of law, some progress was made at the international level to develop new global institutions to promote human rights accountability. The United Nations created a War Crimes Tribunal to prosecute those responsible for gross violations of human rights in much of the former Yugoslavia.

Following the recommendation of the World Conference on

Human Rights, the U.N. General Assembly established the office of High Commissioner for Human Rights with a mandate to remove obstacles to citizens' full enjoyment of basic human rights. The World Conference also recommended establishing a Special Rapporteur on Violence Against Women. The Human Rights Commission will soon take up this project.

Meanwhile, the U.N. Human Rights Center had rapporteurs assess conditions in countries such as Burma, Iraq and Cuba, where human rights are largely disregarded. Other bodies, such as the Committee Against Torture, monitored compliance with U.N. treaties and conventions.

2

HUMAN RIGHTS:
AN OVERVIEW

DEFINING TORTURE

Linda Valerian

Linda Valerian is the director of volunteer services at the Center for the Victims of Torture. The Center is a private nonprofit organization which was founded to provide direct care to survivors of politically motivated torture and their family members. The Center for Victims of Torture is located at 717 East River Road, Minneapolis, Minnesota 55455, phone: 612-626-1400, fax: 612-626-2465.

Points to Consider:

1. How widespread is torture in the modern world?

2. Discuss the meaning and definition of torture.

3. Why is torture used by most nations in the world?

4. How does the United Nations define torture?

5. What is the distinction between physical and psychological torture?

Excerpted from a position paper written by Linda Valerian, "When Refugees Are Victims of Torture," November 1994. Reprinted by permission of Linda Valerian.

Torture has been described as psychological murder or the complete 'unmaking' of the individual.

Amnesty International, the highly respected human rights organization, documents that torture occurs in approximately 100 countries throughout the world. The purpose of torture as a strategic political tool is to control entire populations through terror and intimidation. Torture is used to neutralize real or imagined political opposition and to tyrannize the rest of the population into a state of utter submission.

The prevalence of the use of torture by governments is in part a reflection of widespread adherence to the political doctrine of national security, a state of siege mentality in which all segments of the national population are conceived of as potential security threats. In this context, all people–men, women, children, the elderly, the infirm–are considered potential enemies of the state and are therefore suspect...

In this environment of paranoia and suspicion, with each person considered to be a potential enemy of the state, all aspects of life are politicized. In other words, there is no neutral ground. The way persons dress, the language they speak, their ethnic heritage, their religious affiliation, their work, literally every facet of life is interpreted by the repressive government as being either in agreement with its policies or in opposition to its policies. Arbitrary arrest, detention, and torture are commonplace, and since it is believed that any member of the population is a potential enemy, no one is safe from such abuse. Children, peasant workers, health and religious workers, the elderly, students, and farmers are just as vulnerable to detention and torture as are political opposition leaders.

STATE SECURITY

Torture is used as a strategic component of state security systems to achieve broad political ends through the victimization of individuals. While the overriding purpose of torture is to control, this goal is achieved on an individual basis by attempting to destroy the victims' connection to themselves and to others. This occurs when, under torture, victims are forced to act or react in ways that are so much in conflict with their vision of themselves, in terms of their humanity, their cultural norms, gender roles, spiritual values, professional roles, etc., that they are no longer able to

16

Cartoon by Jeff MacNelly. Reprinted with permission: **Tribune Media Services**.

recognize or know themselves or the world at large.

The United Nations defines torture as "any act by which severe pain or suffering, whether physical or mental, is intentionally inflicted on a person." The definition goes on to describe conditions under which torture may occur, and condemns them all: in order to obtain information from the victim or a third person, in order to punish or intimidate the victim or a third person, or for any reason based upon discrimination of any kind.

It is important to underscore two elements in this definition of torture. The first is that it is somewhat artificial to make a distinction between the physical and the psychological suffering caused by torture. There always is psychological pain as a result of physical torture, and it is common for people of virtually all cultures to express psychological pain physically, through headaches, backaches, skin ailments, gastrointestinal problems, etc. The intention of the United Nations definitions is not so much to separate the experiences of physical versus emotional pain, it is rather to validate the significance of psychological torture. As human rights monitoring groups become increasingly more sophisticated in documenting torture, repressive governments become more creative in perpetrating torture that leaves no physical scars. Since there is no apparent physical damage caused by psychological

17

THE PUNISHMENT

(Rigoberta Menchu won the nobel prize in 1992 for her resistance to the Guatemalan dictatorship. The following quote describes the murder of her family by the oligarchy.)

We walked for one day and almost the whole night to get to the town. Hundreds of soldiers had gathered the people to witness what they were going to do. After a while a truck arrived with 20 people who had been tortured in different ways...We were crying, but almost all the rest of people were crying also at the sight of the tortured people. The army had pulled my little brother's fingernails out, cut off parts of his ears and other parts of his body, his lips, and he was covered with scars and swollen all over. Among the prisoners was a woman and parts of her breasts and other parts of her body were cut off... After three hours, the officer ordered the troops to strip the prisoners and said, "Part of the punishment is still to come." He ordered them tied to some posts. The people didn't know what to do and my mother was overcome with despair. And none of us knew how we could bear the situation. The officer ordered the prisoners covered with gasoline and they set fire to them, one by one.

Excerpted from an autobiographical chapter in "You Can't Drown The Fire: Latin American Women Writing in Exile," by Rigoberta Menchu.

torture, it is often assumed to be less damaging that physical brutality. However, this assumption is not true...

DELIBERATE NATURE

The second element of the United Nations definition of torture to be underscored describes the most critical aspect of torture which sets it apart from other types of trauma: it is deliberate. Torture is the strategic attempt to cause extreme suffering; it is the strategic attempt to destroy an individual. Torture is well planned and well thought out. It is entirely premeditated and intentional. Torture victims experience the horrifying reality of being placed at the mercy of people who have been trained to have no recognition of their humanity and therefore no empathy for their suffering. The powerlessness and isolation of the victim is exacerbated by the fact that the perpetrators are government-sanctioned and government-employed, leaving no hope for rescue, and often marking the victim and his family members to be shunned by a terrorized community.

COMMON FORMS OF TORTURE INCLUDE:

Physical assaults:

Beating, slapping, kicking, or punching

Blows with objects

Falanga (beating on the soles of the feet)

Exposure to extreme cold or heat

Prolonged enforced standing

Hanging, suspension, stretching

Blows to ears

Burning

Electric shocks

Near suffocation

Sexual assault/rape

Deprivation:

Deprived of food

Incommunicado detention or isolation

Restricted movement, immobilization

Blindfolding, total darkness

Lack of needed medication or medical care

Lack of water

Overcrowding

Sleep deprivation

Lack of hygiene

Psychological assaults:

Threats against person

Threats against family, loved ones, colleagues

Witnessing torture of others

Tortured persons put in client's cell

Release and immediate re-arrest

Fluctuation in interrogator's/ torturer's attitude

Verbal abuse

False accusations

Abuse with excrement

Forced choices

Mock execution

Sexual abuse

Sensory over-stimulation:

Constant noise

Screams and voices

Forced ingestion of drugs

Powerful lights

Special devices

3

HUMAN RIGHTS:
AN OVERVIEW

TREATING THE VICTIMS OF TORTURE

Center for the Victims of Torture

The Center for the Victims of Torture in Minneapolis, Minnesota, was the first center of its kind in the United States to provide direct psychological and medical care for survivors of torture.

Points to Consider:

1. What is the Center for Victims of Torture?

2. How was the Center founded?

3. Explain the purpose of torture.

4. Discuss the nature of care and treatment provided for torture victims at the Center.

5. What different professional people does the Center employ to treat victims?

Excerpted from a Center for the Victims of Torture Fact Sheet, 1994.

"They told me, 'You'll be alone with this for the rest of your life. You'll die with this alone.' But when I heard about The Center, I knew the torturers had lied."

The Center for Victims of Torture (CVT) started with the desire of former Minnesota Governor Rudy Perpich to have an impact in the area of human rights. His staff contacted local human rights expert Professor David Weissbrodt, of the University of Minnesota Lawyers International Human Rights Committee. They came up with a list of ten projects, ranging from gathering signatures for a petition in opposition to torture to actually starting a center for treating victims of torture.

Governor Perpich, with characteristic flair, adopted them all. His support helped gain funding from the Northwest Area Foundation which was crucial in getting the center started. So was born the Center for Victims of Torture, the first of its kind in the country and only the third in the world. (The first center was in Copenhagen, the second in Toronto.)

The Center started providing services at the International Clinic of St. Paul-Ramsey in 1985. As a result of that experience, the physicians recommended that the Center move to a stand-alone, less institutional setting that would be less intimidating to refugees and promote the Center's care goals. The center worked on a referral system until the University of Minnesota donated the Center's first home, dedicated in May of 1987. Since then, it has treated more than 400 clients.

The Center moved into its current home at 717 East River Road, also donated by the University of Minnesota, in January of 1991. The new building was renovated with the donations and kind contributions of many local businesses, large and small. With its staff of nine full-time and twenty part-time employees, the Center currently treats approximately 120-150 people per year. That number will increase as additional funds become available.

Care is provided on an outpatient basis only, by an interdiscipli-nary team that includes physicians, nurses, psychiatrists, psychol-ogists and social workers. Treatment is tailored to meet individual client needs, and frequently includes medical treatment, psy-chotherapy, and assistance in gaining economic and legal stabili-ty. Because the Center treats only those who have suffered gov-

322 EIGHTH AVENUE NEW YORK, NEW YORK 10001

ernment-sponsored torture, most of the clients are originally from other countries. The Minnesota Human Rights Advocates provide the Center's clients with legal assistance when necessary.

TORTURE DESTROYS

CVT is founded on the belief that torture can be stopped. Healing survivors is the first step. The purpose of torture is to destroy individuals: physically, emotionally, spiritually. Torture survivors come to The Center for Victims of Torture (CVT) with punctured ear drums and crippled joints, with depression and nightmares, with a lack of trust and deep fears. Their inner strengths have been disassembled by the brutal application of pain, their links to others severed by the strategic use of fear. Their roots of religion, family, and professional values have been destroyed and often turned against them.

The broad message of torture is this: everyone is vulnerable. However perverse the form, the intent of torture is to render the victim powerless by destroying determination, hope, and the

22

capacity to act. Torture has no particular ideology. It is a powerful, isolating tool of repression, the most effective weapon against democracy.

Over 200,000 survivors of government-sponsored torture now live in the United States. As many as 30 percent of refugees are torture victims. More than 8,000 survivors now live in Minnesota alone. Their ongoing pain–and their hope for recovery–is intimately linked with the health and future of our communities.

THE HEALING MISSION

CVT is the first treatment center in the U.S. specifically designed for torture survivors. Started in Minneapolis, Minnesota, in 1985, it remains the only comprehensive, staffed facility in the country. Internationally recognized as a leader in developing and providing effective services to support and heal torture survivors, CVT has served hundreds of torture survivors from over 30 nations of origin.

Because torture attacks the whole person, the process of recovery and healing must also support the whole person. Each new client receives a comprehensive, multidisciplinary assessment from all the healing professionals maintained on staff.

• **Primary Care Physicians** who understand the physical effects of torture, including longterm malnutrition and other disease associated with prolonged imprisonment and deprivation.

• **Psychiatrists** who monitor clinical depressions and emergencies, and prescribe medications to help the survivor begin to control disabling symptoms, such as nightmares.

• **Psychotherapists** who help the survivor control symptoms and assist the longterm healing processes.

• **Social Workers** who assure a safe place to live and support the survivor's relearning of how to participate in the community.

• **Nurses** to monitor case management and provide health care education for survivors and their families.

The work of these highly trained professionals is reinforced with an active community of volunteers that supports the survivors with advocacy, language tutoring, transportation, living support, and friendship. Community volunteers are the ultimate proof that the torturers lied. The healing mission of CVT encompasses treatment, research, training, and public policy advocacy, to expand the resources for the survivors and act against the use of torture.

THE CENTER FOR VICTIMS OF TORTURE:

• Conducts research to understand the longterm effects of torture and what can be done to restore the health and well being of survivors.

• Trains other care professionals nationally and internationally to recognize the symptoms of torture and provides effective treatment.

• Leverages policy decisions that work against international torture.

Through these efforts, CVT is able to treat individual survivors, teach other professionals how to recognize and treat the symptoms of torture, and leverage policy decisions on the national and international level to prevent the use of torture. At CVT, healing allows the survivor to define life goals again and move forward into the future.

A STRATEGIC RESPONSE TO TORTURE

Without help, the effects of torture are long term. They do not stop with the victim, but are passed on from one generation to the next. We've learned from the Holocaust that the disabling symptoms of torture can last a lifetime; even the grandchildren of survivors show higher rates of depression and suicide.

The processes of restoring the health and dignity of survivors undermines the effectiveness of torture as a political weapon. To all of us, attacked by stories of brutality and hopelessness in our world, the healing of survivors can restore the dignity of the human spirit to our communities and ourselves.

4

HUMAN RIGHTS:
AN OVERVIEW

MEDICINE AND HUMAN RIGHTS

Michael A. Grodin, George J. Annas,
and Leonard H. Glantz

*Michael A. Grodin is associate director and George J. Annas is
director of the Law, Medicine and Ethics Program, Boston
University Schools of Medicine and Public Health, Boston,
Massachusetts; Leonard H. Glantz is associate director of the
Boston University School of Public Health.*

Points to Consider:

1. How are crimes against humanity defined?

2. Why is there a need for an international criminal court under
the U.N. to punish crimes against humanity?

3. How do the authors explain the relationship between
medicine and human rights?

4. Explain the nature and meaning of the "Nazi Doctor's Trial."

5. How does the Nuremberg Code apply to doctors?

Michael A. Grodin, George J. Annas and Leonard H. Glantz, "Medicine and
Human Rights: A Proposal for International Action," **Hastings Center Report**,
July/August 1993. Reproduced by permission. © **The Hastings Center.**

Almost half of all German physicians joined the Nazi Party.

Medical ethics is properly viewed as universal, and use of the art of medicine to benefit individual patients is its core. There is also universal condemnation of physicians who engage in "crimes against humanity" such as torture, killing, and involuntary human experimentation under government auspices. Although one need not be a physician to commit crimes against humanity, physicians who commit such acts betray the central ethos of their profession, which should work assiduously to prevent or punish such conduct. Calls for an international criminal code and an international tribunal to judge those accused of crimes against humanity and war crimes have been heard for the past forty years. Nonetheless, there has been no international criminal court established since the post-World War II Nuremberg and Tokyo war crimes trials, and no international codification of crimes against humanity since 1950. A recent United Nations resolution called for an international court to punish war crimes in the former Yugoslavia, but the permanent members of the Security Council oppose the establishment of a permanent international criminal court. *(Editor's Note: In 1994, the U.N. created a War Crimes Tribunal to prosecute war criminals in the former Yugoslavia.)*

CRIMINAL COURT

We support those who continue to work for a permanent international criminal court under United Nations auspices designed to punish human rights abuses that can properly be designated crimes against humanity. Nevertheless, we recognize that it may be decades before the international community agrees to establish such a tribunal. Rather than waiting for this perhaps ideal approach to materialize, we believe it is time for the physicians and lawyers of the world, as the two major professions dedicated to promoting human welfare and human rights, to take concrete steps to prevent governments from using physicians as instruments of killing, torture, persecution (on racial, political, or religious grounds), and involuntary human experimentation. Such deterrence requires a clear statement of prohibited conduct, a mechanism for punishing those who engage in such conduct and for supporting those who resist.

HISTORICAL CONTEXT

The 1946-1947 trial of Nazi doctors (the "Doctors' Trial") documented the most notorious example of physician participation in human rights abuses, criminal activities, and murder. Hitler called upon physicians not only to help justify his racial hatred policies with a "scientific" rationale (racial hygiene), but also to direct his euthanasia programs and ultimately his death camps. Almost half of all German physicians joined the Nazi Party. In his opening statement at the Doctors' Trial, General Telford Taylor, the chief prosecutor, spoke to the watershed nature of the trial for the history of medical ethics and law:

It is our deep obligation to all peoples of the world to show why and how these things happened. It is incumbent upon us to set forth with conspicuous clarity the ideas and motives which moved these defendants to treat their fellow men as less than beasts. The perverse thoughts and distorted concepts which brought about these savageries are not dead. They cannot be killed by force of arms. They must not become a spreading cancer in the breast of humanity. They must be cut out and exposed, for the reasons so well stated by Mr. Justice Jackson in the courtroom a year ago [before the War Crimes Tribunal]: "The wrongs which we seek to condemn and punish have been so calculated, so malignant, and so devastating, that civilization cannot tolerate their being ignored because it cannot survive their being repeated."

Sixteen physician-scientists were found guilty, and seven executed, on the basis of international and natural law. A universal standard of physician responsibility in human rights abuses involving experimentation on humans, the Nuremberg Code, was articulated and has been widely recognized, if not always followed, by the world community.

The Nuremberg Code was a response to the horrors of Nazi experimentation in the death camps–experimentation on a wide scale, without consent, that often had the death of the prisoner-subject as its planned endpoint. The code has ten provisions, two designed to protect the rights of human subjects of experimentation, and eight designed to protect their welfare...

NUREMBERG

Although the Nuremberg Code has not been adopted as a whole by the United Nations, its consent principle did become an important part of the United Nations International Covenant on Civil and Political Rights, which was promulgated in 1966 and adopted by the United Nations General Assembly in 1974. Article 7 of the Covenant states:

No one shall be subjected to torture or to cruel, inhuman or degrading treatment or punishment. In particular, no one shall be subjected without his free consent to medical or scientific experimentation.

Most physicians would, of course, be shocked at having anything they do to patients be considered "torture or cruel, inhuman or degrading treatment." They would thus view the Covenant's provisions much the same way they might view the Nuremberg Code: as a criminal law document not applicable to anything done by physicians. But this is a mistake, and only helps to protect aberrant physicians by marginalizing their actions as nonmedical in nature and therefore of no concern to the medical profession. As Jay Katz has noted, both torture and involuntary human experimentation are assaults on bodily integrity—in their disregard of that integrity, torture and involuntary human experimentation become virtually indistinguishable.

29

5

HUMAN RIGHTS:
AN OVERVIEW

POLITICAL MURDER AND THE
DISAPPEARED

Amnesty International

*Amnesty International is impartial and works to prevent torture
and human rights violations throughout the world. Amnesty
International is independent of any government, political persua-
sion or religious creed. It does not support or oppose any government or political system, nor does it support or oppose the views
of the victims whose rights it seeks to protect. It is concerned
solely with the protection of the human rights involved in each
case, regardless of the ideology of the government or opposition
forces, or the beliefs of the individual.*

Points to Consider:

1. How can the United Nations combat political killings and
   disappearances?

2. What is Amnesty International's 14 point program?

3. How many people have been killed by their governments
   since 1960?

4. Discuss the definition of the term "disappeared."

5. How does Amnesty International define the term
   "political killing?"

"Getting Away with Murder: The Lives Behind the Lies," **Amnesty Action**, Fall 1993.
Reprinted with permission.

Millions of men, women and children have been killed or "disappeared" by their own governments since the 1960s.

Stating that political killings and "disappearances" were the greatest threat to human rights in the 1990s, Amnesty International recently launched "The Lives Behind the Lies," a year-long world-wide campaign to end "disappearances" and political killings.

At a press conference in Washington, D.C. to launch the campaign, Pierre Sané, Secretary General of Amnesty International, said that "hopes that human rights would be respected in the much-heralded 'new world order' have been shot down. Instead, old regimes, newly-formed governments and armed opposition groups are turning their streets into killing grounds or causing their opponents to vanish without trace."

As part of its campaign to end "disappearances" and political killings, Amnesty International is stepping up its call on the United Nations to appoint a High Commissioner for Human Rights with the authority to take urgent action, for increased resources to the UN's human rights program and for the establishment of an impartial, independent international court.

PROGRAMS

The organization is also calling on all governments to implement its 14-point programs for preventing "disappearances" and political killings. "The world must wake up to the continuing mass slaughter," said Sané. "Unless both individual governments and the international community take action soon to end political killings and "disappearances," the rising tide of carnage could overwhelm the institutions set up to protect international human rights after the horrors of the Second World War."

In its 1992 Annual Report, Amnesty International recorded political killings in some 45 countries, and reported that at least 1,270 people in 20 countries "disappeared" after arrest by security forces in 1991. It also reported that in at least 29 countries people who were earlier reported to have "disappeared" have yet to be accounted for sufficiently.

Jabbar Rashid Shifki was just 15 years old when he was arrested by the Iraqi army in 1983. He was one of 8,000 members of the

31

Barzani clan who were rounded up by Iraqi forces during a raid on a resettlement camp in northern Iraq. Their "crime?" They belonged to the "wrong" ethnic group; they were Kurds, believed by the Iraqi Government to be helping Iran in the Iran/Iraq War. Ten years later, the fate and whereabouts of the men and boys, ranging in age from eight to 80, are still unknown.

AI says relatives of the victims of such "disappearances" suffer a particularly cruel fate. They do not know if their husband or wife, brother or sister, child or parent is dead or alive, and many spend years in a fruitless search, unable to rest because they have no definite information. They run up against endless denials from officials who may be, in fact, holding their loved ones. Their difficulties can be made worse by the climate of fear surrounding "disappearances." Witnesses may be too frightened to come forward and give evidence openly. If they do come forward, they may receive threats or "disappear" themselves.

THE DISAPPEARED

Millions of men, women and children have been killed or "disappeared" by their own governments since the 1960s because of their political views or their ethnic origin, because of where they lived, or simply because they were poor.

In Indonesia, half a million people were killed in the 1960s in an "anti-Communist" drive. In the 1970s hundreds of thousands were murdered by the Khmer Rouge in the "killing fields" of Pol Pot's "Democratic" Kampuchea (Cambodia) and thousands of people "disappeared" under Argentina's military juntas in the late 1970s. Things did not improve in the 1980s: up to two percent of the population of El Salvador is estimated to have been wiped out by the government; tens of thousands have "disappeared" in Sri Lanka.

And the end of the Cold War, with democratically-elected governments supposedly replacing military juntas and totalitarian regimes, has not meant the end to the killing and suffering. Tens of thousands of people are still being murdered each year or "disappear" without trace at the hands of government agents. In countries around the world, people live in fear of death or wait to hear about the fate of friends and relatives who have "disappeared."

"The power of the state is increasingly being turned to cold-blooded murder, its officials trained in the skills of the assassin and the kidnapper," said Sané. "These acts–sometimes secret, but often brazen killings and kidnapping with no pretense of legality–fly in the face of international standards and are outlawed even in war."

DEFINITIONS

Amnesty International defines the "disappeared" as people who have been taken into custody, yet whose whereabouts and fate are unknown. Witnesses have usually seen them being detained, but the authorities deny holding them. The safeguards that nor-mally guarantee their safety in custody are suspended. The pris-oner is cut off from the outside world and has no protection. At best, he or she may simply be in unacknowledged detention, unharmed, and may "reappear" in time. Other "disappeared" prisoners are less fortunate; they are tortured, killed, and their bodies disposed of secretly. Other people are killed outright by government or opposition forces.

Marta Crisóstomo García, a 22-year-old nurse, was a witness to one of the worst massacres in Peru in recent memory. In May 1988 some 30 Indian peasants were killed by the army in the small town of Cayara in revenge for an ambush on a military con-voy by the Communist Party of Peru-Shining Path. The military then hunted down and killed witnesses who could testify against them. Marta Crisóstomo gave evidence to the official inquiry.

She soon began to receive death threats, and in September 1989 was shot dead in her house by an army "death squad."

POLITICAL KILLING

Amnesty International defines "political killings" as unlawful and deliberate killings, carried out by order of a government or with its complicity. Sometimes they are reprisal killings, with civilians killed in retaliation for the killing of a security forces officer. Sometimes individual opponents or critics of the government, such as trade union members, human rights activists or religious leaders, are assassinated. Sometimes the killings are public and blatant, as when peaceful demonstrators are killed, as happened in Tiananmen Square, China, in 1989. Sometimes the killings are committed by uniformed officers, in other cases by members of paramilitary forces or plain-clothes "death squads." If security forces are involved, they often try to hide their role by operating in street clothes and using unmarked vehicles. They may blame the opposition for killings they themselves committed or may claim that the victims were killed in shoot-outs or while trying to escape. They may try to legitimize their actions by claiming that the victims were "terrorists."

"Disappearances" and political killings have become the preferred means of dealing with political opponents in many countries, replacing long-term imprisonment, part of a changing global pattern of human rights abuses.

6

HUMAN RIGHTS:
AN OVERVIEW

NATIVE AMERICANS AND HUMAN RIGHTS

Ward Churchill

Ward Churchill has been co-director of Colorado American Indian Movement (AIM) since 1980 and coordinator of American studies at the University of Colorado, Boulder. His books include Marxism and Native Americans, Agents of Repression, The Cointelpro Papers, Critical Issues in Native North America, *and* Fantasies of the Master Race.

Points to Consider:

1. What was the "Columbian Encounter?"

2. How many Indians in the Caribbean Basin became extinct?

3. Explain the use of small pox in the war against Indians.

4. How did Supreme Court decisions help whites take Indian lands?

5. Summarize the meaning of "manifest destiny."

6. By 1890, how many Indians remained alive within the United States?

Ward Churchill, "Since Predator Came," **CovertAction Quarterly**, Spring 1992. This article was reprinted/adapted from **CovertAction Quarterly**, Spring 1992, number 40, 1500 Massachusetts Avenue #732, Washington D.C. 20005, phone (202) 331-9763. Annual subscriptions in the U.S. are $22; Canada $27; Europe $33. The issue of **CovertAction**, containing the full text of the article with footnotes is available from CAQ for $8 in the U.S. and $12 other.

[W]e gave them two blankets and a handkerchief out of the smallpox hospital. I hope it will have the desired effect.

–Lord Jeffrey Amherst

On October 12, 1492, Christopher Columbus, blinded by greed and arrogance, first washed upon a Caribbean beach. Neither then, nor in subsequent landings, did he see what lay before him–a continent rich in culture and civilization.

The exceedingly complex societies of this "New" World had existed on the North American continent continuously for 50,000 years and supported perhaps 15 million people. They had developed highly advanced architecture and engineering; spiritual traditions embodying equivalents to modern ecoscience; refined knowledge of pharmacology and holistic medicine; highly sophisticated systems of governance, trade and diplomacy; and environmentally sound farming procedures out of which originated well over half the modern world's vegetal foodstuffs. The primarily agricultural economies were able to support cities as populous as the 40,000-person center of Cahokia in present-day Illinois.

SOCIAL ORDER

By and large, the societies were organized along extremely egalitarian lines, with real property held collectively. Women shared real political and economic power and matrifocality was a normative standard. War, at least in the Euro-derived sense the term is understood today, was virtually unknown.

Within an astonishingly short period, the face of Native America was changed beyond all recognition. The "Columbian Encounter" unleashed a predatory, five-century-long cycle of European conquest, genocide and colonization. Indeed, over the first decade of Spanish presence in the Caribbean–while Columbus himself was governor–the pattern was set. Slavery and slaughter, combined with the introduction of Old World pathogens, reduced the native Taion population of just one island–Española (presently the Dominican Republic and Haiti)–from as many as eight million to fewer than 100,000 people. By 1542, only 200 could be found by Spanish census-takers. Within a generation, the 14 million Indians of the Caribbean Basin were declared extinct.

Cartoon by Joe Heller.

DISEASE AND EPIDEMICS

In North America, a similar dynamic was set in motion by the 1513 expedition of Ponce de León into Florida. Before the small-pox pandemic it brought had run its course in 1524, the plague spanned the continent and killed about three-quarters of all indigenous people north of the Rîo Grande. This was only the beginning. Between 1520 and 1890, there were no fewer than 41 smallpox epidemics and pandemics among North American Indians. To this number must be added dozens of lethal out-breaks of measles, whooping cough, tuberculosis, bubonic plague, typhus, cholera, typhoid, diphtheria, scarlet fever, pleurisy, mumps, venereal disease and the common cold.

The attrition of native populations by disease has usually been treated as a tragic but wholly inadvertent byproduct of contact between Native Americans and Europeans. The perception by many Indians that the English deliberately employed smallpox as a form of biological warfare is amply documented. In 1763, Lord Jeffrey Amherst told his subordinates to infect the members of Pontiac's Algonquin confederacy "by means of [smallpox-contam-inated] blankets as well as...every other means to extirpate this execrable race."

A few days later, it was reported to Amherst, "[W]e gave them two blankets and a handkerchief out of the smallpox hospital. I hope it will have the desired effect." It did. As an early form of biological warfare, the epidemic that Amherst initiated killed at least 100,000 Native Americans. In 1836, as many as a quarter-million Indians died after the U.S. Army knowingly distributed smallpox-laden blankets among the Missouri River Mandans...

ENTER THE UNITED STATES

Although it renounced rights of conquest and in the 1789 Northwest Ordinance pledged "utmost good faith" in its dealings with Indians, the fledgling U.S. embarked almost immediately on a course of territorial acquisition far more ambitious than that of its colonialist precursors. From 1810 to 1814, a sequence of extremely brutal military campaigns against the Shawnee in the Ohio River Valley, and the Creek Confederacy further south eliminated the Native military capacity east of the Mississippi. The government then forcibly relocated entire indigenous nations and "cleared" the eastern U.S. for repopulation by white "settlers." Attrition was severe; thousands died when the Cherokee were rounded up at bayonet-point and marched over the 1,500-mile "Trail of Tears." This federal "removal policy" would be echoed a century later in Adolf Hitler's *lebensraumpolitik* policy.

The government understood clearly that Indians were an impediment to the expansion of white settlers who would open the land to profit-making productivity. Since these inconvenient Natives could be classified as subhuman savages, the process of controlling and even killing them carried no more moral weight than an exercise in animal husbandry.

MARSHALL DOCTRINE

During the 1820s and 1830s, Chief Justice of the Supreme Court John Marshall penned a series of high court opinions based in large part upon the medieval Doctrine of Discovery. Over the next four decades, the U.S. used this veneer of legality to acquire Indian territory through at least 371 nation-to-nation agreements. In a bizarre departure from established principles of international law, however, Marshall also argued that U.S. sovereignty was inherently "higher" than that of the nations with which it was making treaties. Since Indians had no right to refuse to sell their land to the U.S., any resistance to the appropriation of their territory became an "act of war" which justified a military "response."

By 1903, the "Marshall Doctrine" established "intrinsic" federal "plenary" (full) power over all Indians within the U.S., and released the government from its treaty obligations while leaving the land title gained through those treaties intact. In conjunction with this novel notion of international jurisprudence, the high court ruled that the government enjoyed "natural" and permanent "trust" prerogatives over all residual Native property.

INVOKING MANIFEST DESTINY

Having consolidated its grip east of the Mississippi during the 1840s and having militarily seized "rights" to the northern half of Mexico as well, the U.S. proclaimed its "Manifest Destiny" to expand west to the Pacific. Indian-controlled land had no part in this agenda. The ensuing rhetoric of outright extermination by both federal policymakers and a sizable segment of the public led unerringly to a lengthy and extensive chain of massacres of

Indians in the Great Plains and Basin regions by U.S. troops. Among the worst were the slaughters perpetrated at Blue River (Nebraska, 1854), Bear River (Idaho, 1863), Sand Creek (Colorado, 1864), Washita River (Oklahoma, 1868), Sappa Creek (Kansas, 1875), Camp Robinson (Nebraska, 1878) and Wounded Knee (South Dakota, 1890). According to the Census Bureau, by 1894, in barely a century, the U.S. had waged "more than 40" separate wars against Native people killing a "very much greater" number than the Bureau's figure of 30,000.

LIQUIDATION

The "quite substantial" indigenous death toll from "private actions" during U.S. continental expansion was in all probability far higher than the formal military toll. In California alone, the Native population was reduced from approximately 300,000 in 1800 to fewer than 20,000 in 1890, "chiefly [because of] the cruelties and wholesale massacres perpetrated by...miners and the early settlers." In Texas, where a bounty was placed on any Indian scalp brought to a government office, North America's most diverse Native population was "exterminated or brought to the brink of extinction by [Euroamerican civilians] who often had no more regard for the life of an Indian than they had for that of a dog, sometimes less."

After the indigenous population was virtually liquidated, its agricultural economy destroyed and its remaining food sources–most notably the buffalo–wiped out, white settlers took over most of their land. By 1890, less than 5 percent, or fewer than 250,000 Indians, remained alive within the U.S. The survivors were lodged on a patchwork of "reservations" even then being dismantled through application of the 1887 "General Allotment Act."

Under this formal eugenics code, those who could prove "one-half or more degree of Indian blood" and accepted U.S. citizenship typically received 160 acres or less. Reservation land remaining after each person with sufficient "blood quantum" had received his or her allotment was declared "surplus." By 1930, government-certified Indians were concentrated in about 2.5 percent of their original holdings–fifty million arid or semi-arid acres–while the best 100 million acres were stripped away and opened up to non-Indian homesteading, corporate acquisition, or conversion into national parks and forests. This model was later borrowed by the apartheid government of South Africa for its "racial homeland" system of territorial apportionment...

TREATIES

Europeans began taking their land in the form of treaties. The manner in which those treaties were handled might be summarized by means of the first of them: the 1805 agreement in which the United States acquired from the Dakota 100,000 acres in what is now the Minneapolis and St. Paul Twin Cities area.

Lt. Zebulon Pike, known for Pike's Peak, valued the land at $200,000. The U.S. Senate authorized that $2,000 be spent. The Dakota present at the signing received $200 and some liquor.

David Peterson, "American Indians in Minnesota," **Star Tribune**, June 12, 1990.

DOMINATION

For grassroots Indian people, the broader human costs of ongoing U.S. domination are devastating. The 1.6 million American Indians within the U.S. remain, nominally at least, the largest per capita land owners in North America. Given the extent of the resources within their land base, Indians should logically be the continent's wealthiest "ethnic group." Instead, according to the federal government's own statistics, they are the poorest with far and away the lowest annual and lifetime incomes, the highest rate of unemployment, the lowest rate of pay when employed, and the lowest level of educational attainment of any North American population aggregate. Correspondingly, they suffer, by decisive margins, the greatest incidence of malnutrition and diabetes, death by exposure, tuberculosis, infant mortality, plague disease, and similar maladies. These conditions, combined with the general disempowerment which spawns them, breed an unremitting sense of rage, frustration and despair which is reflected by spiraling rates of domestic and other forms of intra-group violence, alcoholism and resulting death by accident or fetal alcohol syndrome. Consequently, in an extraordinarily telling measure of the stark reality of conditions, the average life expectancy of a reservation-based Native American male in 1980 was a mere 44.6 years, that of his female counterpart less than three years longer. Such a statistical portrait is more representative of the Third World poor than of landowners in a wealthy and industrialized state.

41

7

HUMAN RIGHTS:
AN OVERVIEW

THE WORLD'S INDIGENOUS PEOPLES

Julian Burger

Julian Burger is responsible for the indigenous peoples program at the United Nations Center for Human Rights. He is the author of Gaia Atlas of First Peoples: A Future for the Indigenous World *(Anchor Books, 1990) and* Report from the Frontier: The State of the World's Indigenous Peoples *(Zed Books, 1987). The views in this article do not necessarily reflect those of the United Nations.*

Points to Consider:

1. How is the current global status of indigenous peoples described?

2. Explain the consequences of colonialism on indigenous peoples.

3. Summarize the contemporary relationship between resources, land and indigenous peoples.

4. Analyze the meaning of the U.N. Draft Declaration on the Rights of Indigenous Peoples.

Julian Burger, "An International Agenda," from the book **State of the Peoples: A Global Human Rights Report on Societies in Danger**, by Cultural Survival, 1993. Reprinted with permission.

In Amazonia and several Asian countries, poor farmers, squeezed off their own lands by agro-industry, have migrated in massive numbers onto indigenous peoples' territory.

The historical record is familiar. No one doubts the fateful impact on the indigenous peoples of the Americas of what UNESCO ingenuously calls the "encounter of two cultures." It was a human disaster. The story of the Americas is duplicated in other regions subjected to the scourge of European colonialism: Australia, New Zealand, the Pacific, Africa, and Asia, including the vast area in the East and North of the former Soviet Union.

The legacy of that history in the day-to-day life of indigenous peoples cannot be ignored. Consider official government statistics. In New Zealand, indigenous peoples are 7 times more likely to be unemployed than the average person; 50 percent of prisoners are Maaori, although Maaori make up only 9 percent of the population. In Australia, Aboriginal peoples have a life expectancy 20 years less than the average and are 14 times more likely to go to prison. Indigenous peoples make up over 60 percent of Guatemala's population but only 150 out of the 25,000 students are in higher education. In Canada, infant mortality among indigenous peoples is over twice the national average.

COLONIALISM

These consequences of colonialism are one reason why so many indigenous peoples want the international community to take action. But there is another reason, perhaps even more critical. Indigenous peoples are victims of a modern-day colonialism, driven by humanity's determination to know all, explore all, exploit all. The insistent impulse to turn the planet into an interlinked whole, with global production, marketing, and communications, has brought a powerful, impatient world to the doorsteps of indigenous peoples.

As more accessible resources are exhausted, the search for raw materials escalates in comparatively neglected regions. Indigenous peoples sit on some of the world's last remaining natural resources, and both the rich countries of the North and the elites of the developing nations of the South want to exploit these stores, perhaps for legitimate development but just as likely for the profit of distant shareholders. At the same time, as the world pop-

43

Cartoon by David Seavey. Copyright 1989, **USA Today**, reprinted with permission.

ulation soars well past 5 billion people, pressure rises to open up potential living spaces.

LAND AND RESOURCES

Contemporary colonialism is devastating the everyday lives of indigenous peoples. In the quest for resources and land, the great wildernesses have become El Dorados and escape valves. Few of the 50 million indigenous inhabitants of the world's rain forests–who depend on it for food, medicine, shelter, and income–have escaped the assault of loggers, settlers, miners, and dam-builders. In Amazonia and several Asian countries, poor farmers, squeezed off their own lands by agro-industry, have migrated in massive numbers onto indigenous peoples' territory. Today, the indigenous peoples of Amazonia are outnumbered 16 to one. By early in the next century, Indonesia plans to move up

44

10 million people from Java to indigenous lands on the outer islands.

Mining and large-scale hydroelectric schemes threaten to displace, or have already displaced, hundreds of thousands of indigenous and tribal peoples. For example, a series of dams on India's Sardar Sarovar River imperils nearly 100,000 people, most of whom are tribals. Under the government's plans, many people will be removed and receive virtually no land or monetary compensation, and will probably end up swelling the already vast unemployed and marginalized slum-dwelling population in towns. And India's dam project is but one of many that are changing the lives of indigenous peoples throughout the world.

U.N. DRAFT DECLARATION ON THE RIGHTS OF INDIGENOUS PEOPLES

Often denied recognition of their concerns in the countries where they live, indigenous peoples are asking the international community to extend and guarantee their rights. Once neglected and excluded from international forums, indigenous peoples are pursuing a number of possibilities for political action in this domain...

When adopted by the General Assembly, the draft declaration will form the basis for a new relationship of indigenous peoples with states and with the United Nations. Perhaps most important, it states that "Indigenous peoples have the right to autonomy and self-government in matters relating to their internal and local affairs." The document affirms the right of indigenous peoples to self-determination and to control their lands and resources. It emphasizes the right of indigenous peoples to determine membership in their societies, establish their own institutions according to their own practices, and retain and develop their own customs, laws, and legal systems. And it asserts the right of indigenous peoples to maintain their differences and determine their future collectively.

The draft declaration specifically recognizes the right of indigenous peoples to protection against cultural genocide, defined as any form of forced assimilation or deprivation of their distinct cultural characteristics. Paralleling this right, the draft declaration includes the right to the protection of sacred sites, the restitution of cultural property, and the repatriation of human remains.

OPPRESSION

Slaughtered, forcibly deported, ravaged by disease, marginalized economically and politically, often reduced to cruel caricatures by our popular culture, the indigenous peoples of the Americas have existed in the shadows of our collective consciousness for 500 years.

Tracy Thomas, "We Have Always Lived Here," **Amnesty Action**, Summer/Fall, 1992.

CONTROL AND ACCESS

The draft declaration also incorporates principles of greater access to and control over public services. Broadly speaking, there are two reasons indigenous peoples fare far worse than any other group according to every socioeconomic indicator: a lack of access to services (sometimes as a result of discrimination) and the delivery of services that are inappropriate, alien, or culturally unacceptable. The draft declaration amplifies what some countries have made official policy: a system of services that indigenous peoples themselves plan and implement.

Indeed, times have changed dramatically since the United Nations held the first World Conference on Human Rights in 1968. At that time, the term "indigenous peoples" wasn't even part of the language; indigenous peoples were considered a remnant of the past, destined to an inexorable assimilation into mainstream societies. In 1993, by contrast, the Second World Conference on Human Rights asked the General Assembly to proclaim a decade for indigenous peoples. Just as this International Year of the World's Indigenous Peoples has generated public support for the rights of indigenous peoples, a decade of commitment to their rights and well-being would provide a framework for the next chapter of progress for indigenous peoples.

8

HUMAN RIGHTS:
AN OVERVIEW

RAPE AND SEXUAL ABUSE
IN CUSTODY

Amnesty Action

Amnesty Action *is the newsletter of Amnesty International.*

Points to Consider:

1. Why do state officials in many nations often use rape and sexual abuse against women in custody?

2. Why is rape defined as a form of torture?

3. Which women are usually singled out for rape and sexual abuse?

4. How do officials often get away with rape and sexual abuse?

"Against Their Will: Rape and Sexual Abuse in Custody," **Amnesty Action**, January/February 1992. Reprinted with permission.

Women who are active politically can be special targets for rape or sexual abuse in custody.

May 18, 1990 was Mubina Gani's wedding day. She can still recall the events of that day in detail. They aren't pleasant memories. It was near midnight when the 18-year-old bride and her wedding party of 27, traveling by bus, approached a border checkpoint near Badasgam Village in Kashmir, India.

The checkpoint was manned by soldiers of the Border Security Forces. As the bus rolled to a halt, soldiers unexpectedly opened fire, killing the bridegroom's brother instantly and wounding nine others, including Mubina Gani and her new husband. When the shooting had ended, the soldiers entered the bus.

"We lay down under the seats and pretended to be dead," she said. "They came inside and started to beat everyone." Some of the guards dragged the bride and her pregnant aunt into a nearby field. "We were crying bitterly," she recounted. "I told them I had not seen my husband. But they didn't listen. They took off our clothes...and we were raped. Four to six men raped me, I think." Suffering from shock and gunshot wounds, Mubina Gani was taken into military custody. They held her there for 48 hours.

When news of this incident initially leaked out, Indian officials maintained that the bus had been caught in a crossfire. However, a Superintendent of Police later confirmed that the border guards had opened fire on the bus without provocation and that two women had been gang-raped at the scene. In the aftermath of the incident, four soldiers were suspended from duty, but no further legal action appears to have been taken.

GOVERNMENT AGENTS

What made this case unusual was the fact that it gained any notoriety at all. In fact, rape and sexual abuse by government agents of women in custody is common in many countries according to information gathered by Amnesty International. Rape and sexual abuse have long been powerful weapons used by state officials to abuse, coerce, humiliate, punish and intimidate women.

"When policemen or soldiers rape a woman in their custody, that act is no longer an act of private violence, but an act of torture or ill-treatment for which the state bears responsibility," says

48

FEMALE SEXUAL SLAVERY

"Lin Lin" is just one of thousands of Burmese women and girls who have been trafficked and sold into what amounts to female sexual slavery in Thailand. In the last two years, Thai NGOs estimate that at a minimum, some twenty thousand Burmese women and girls are suffering Lin Lin's fate, or worse, and that ten thousand new recruits come in every year. They are moved from one brothel to another as the demand for new faces dictates, and often end up being sent back to Burma after a year or two to recruit their own successors.

These Burmese women and girls are only a fraction of the estimated 800,000 to two million prostitutes currently working in Thailand. We focus this report on the Burmese trafficking victims because of the range of violations of internationally-recognized human rights that they suffer, from debt bondage to arbitrary detention, and because government officials, particularly from Thailand, are complicit in these violations both by direct involvement in the brothels and by failing to enforce Thailand's obligation under both national and international law.

Excerpted from "A Modern Forum of Slavery: Trafficking of Burmese Women and Girls into Brothels in Thailand," **Asia Watch** (New York: Human Rights Watch), p. 1, 1993.

Sheila Dauer of Amnesty International USA's Women's Program Steering Committee, which coordinates the section's work for women. What Amnesty has frequently found, however, is yawning government indifference to rape as a human rights issue and even outright legal hostility to rape victims.

An Amnesty International delegation touring Peru in 1986 was told point blank by a prosecutor that rape was to be expected during counter-insurgency operations and that the organization should not expect prosecutions. For years the organization has compiled cases of dozens of rapes of young women and teenage girls by soldiers operating in special security zones in the Peruvian mountains.

PUNISHMENT

Even when public outrage forces an investigation or prosecution, punishments imposed by courts on government agents seldom fit the crime. In 1989 three police officers repeatedly raped a 30-year-old widow at a police facility in Indonesia. The rape soon became known in the woman's home village and irate villagers stormed the police station in Geumpang Aceh, where the rape took place. The villagers had to be forcibly dispersed by soldiers from a local military base.

In the aftermath of the incident the local chief of police promised an investigation. The three officers were ultimately tried before a military court. Two of them received seven-month sentences and were dismissed from the force. The third was sentenced to one year, but was not dismissed from the force because he was due for retirement.

Women's groups in the Philippines have reported extensively on the rape and sexual abuse of women detained during military operations there. The victims have included human rights workers, members of legal, political, or social organizations, and women living in villages where there is suspected rebel activity.

Women who are active politically or involved in community programs or human rights work can be special targets for rape or sexual abuse in custody. But in remote areas under military control, where rape frequently becomes a form of recreation for bored soldiers, all women are vulnerable.

INTERROGATION

Rape and sexual abuse frequently take place in custody during interrogation. The interrogators may be after something specific, like information or a signature on a confession, or they simply might want to frighten the victim and other local women.

Rose Ann Maguire was arrested in July 1991 in Northern Ireland and held five days in Casteleagh Interrogation Center. During one session she was reportedly sexually harassed. A detective fondled her breast and put his hand between her legs. She was also physically abused, slapped, and threatened with death. She was later released without charge.

The feeling of isolation that any rape victim feels is compounded when the rapist is a government agent. Many women believe it is futile to bring charges against their violators, because in many cases they would be talking to the same power structure. A 14-

year-old girl, who was repeatedly raped by three soldiers in the Philippines in January 1991, filed criminal charges at the Office of the Provincial Prosecutor. Although witness statements and a medical report supported her allegations, no action has ever been taken against her attackers.

LITTLE JUSTICE

If the justice system offers little redress for rape victims in some countries, there are others where the justice system in effect puts rape victims in a classic and cruel Catch-22 situation. Under Pakistan's Hudood Ordinance, a woman convicted of extramarital sexual relations–including rape–can be sentenced to be publicly whipped, imprisoned, or stoned to death. In August 1991 two nurses were raped at gunpoint by three interns at Karachi Hospital. One of the nurses tried to file a complaint and was herself charged with admitting to sexual intercourse. As a result of these charges, she has lost her job, and her marital engagement has been broken off. "No one else can ever know how I feel inside," she says. "I may seem all right on the outside, but on the inside I feel as if I no longer exist."

FOUR STEPS TO PREVENT RAPE AND SEXUAL ABUSE

Amnesty International has established a four-step program to ensure that the human rights of women are protected. Because, although men are sometimes raped in police or military custody, this is a form of torture primarily suffered by women and to which women are uniquely vulnerable.

1. Make Government Policy Clear

Government officials must publicly emphasize that rape and sexual abuse by government agents are grave and intolerable human rights violations. Military, police, and security personnel must be advised that anyone who commits human rights violations will be brought to justice.

2. Implement Safeguards

Female police personnel or guards must be present during interrogation of female detainees and prisoners. Statements or confessions extracted as a result of torture or ill-treatment–including rape–must never be admitted in legal proceedings.

All forms of detention or imprisonment must be supervised and controlled by judicial authorities. All detainees and prisoners must be given prompt and regular access to family members and legal counsel. Detainees and prisoners must be held in officially recognized detention centers. There should be no contact between male guards and female detainees unless a female guard is present. Any female detainee who alleges that she has been raped must be given an immediate medical examination, preferably by a female doctor.

3. Investigate and Prosecute

All reports of rape, sexual harassment and other forms of torture or cruel, inhuman, or degrading treatment must be promptly, thoroughly, and impartially investigated. All soldiers, policemen, or other government agents who commit, encourage, or condone rape and sexual harassment or any other human rights abuse must be brought to justice.

4. Compensate and Rehabilitate

Governments must provide victims of torture and ill-treatment–including rape and sexual abuse in custody–with rehabilitative medical treatment and financial compensation.

9

HUMAN RIGHTS:
AN OVERVIEW

GENOCIDE IN BOSNIA

Roger P. Winter

Roger P. Winter has been the director of the United States Committee for Refugees (USCR). He wrote the following statement based on first hand observations of the USCR staff members doing humanitarian work with refugees and displaced persons in and outside of Bosnia and Herzegovina. USCR is a program of the American Council for Nationalities Service.

Points to Consider:

1. How many Bosnians have been displaced by the civil war?

2. Why have actions by the Serb forces been described as genocide?

3. What is meant by ethnic cleansing?

4. Explain the legal status of Bosnian refugees in Croatia, Slovenia and Hungary.

Excerpted from congressional testimony by Roger P. Winter before the U.S. Commission on Security and Cooperation in Europe (Helsinki Commission), January 25, 1993.

REFUGEES AND DISPLACED PERSONS

Bosnia and Herzegovina, which had a population of 4.4 million in April 1992, has been devastated by the attacks that followed U.S. and European Community recognition of Bosnian independence. Although exact figures are not available, nearly one-half of all Bosnians–some two million people–are believed to have lost or been forced from their homes. This includes about half the entire pre-conflict Muslim population. About 1.1 million have sought refuge outside Bosnia, within former Yugoslavia, in Croatia, Slovenia, Macedonia and Serbia, as well as in other European states, principally Germany, Hungary, Sweden, Austria, and Switzerland. An estimated 810,000 are internally displaced within Bosnia (or refugees from earlier fighting in Croatia who fled to Bosnia), in especially grave danger, bearing the brunt of a harsh winter with inadequate food, clothing, medicine, and shelter, and still at imminent risk of extreme violence. Serbian forces in Bosnia have systematically destroyed the homes of Muslims who were forcibly displaced, making their eventual return all the more difficult and the extent of loss all the greater. Serb civilians from western Herzegovina have also abandoned their homes, some of which, in areas of Croat control, have also been destroyed. Serbs have also fled Sarajevo, fearing reprisals as well as shelling. Some 271,000 persons have fled from Bosnia and Herzegovina to Serbia.

PEACE

Recent overtures towards the Geneva peace proposals from the self-styled Serbian parliament must be welcomed, but not overly valued. So long as the Serbian siege of Sarajevo continues, actions will speak far louder than words. A real ceasefire must be a pre-condition for real negotiations. Any autonomy plan must include the right of displaced persons and refugees to return to their homes and/or to be compensated for their losses. Any plan must also include firm guarantees for the protection of minorities and respect for human rights. Without adequate provisions for international enforcement, however, the outlook for successful implementation of a peace plan is dim.

Whatever progress is made at the peace table may take a long time to be felt on the ground. Movement on the diplomatic front should in no way result in a hands-off attitude on the part of the international community with regard to ongoing allegations of

Cartoon by Richard Wright.

atrocities and obstruction of humanitarian assistance. Any letting up of pressure would send precisely the wrong signal to those eager to continue their aggression and realize expansionist goals. The international community must attend immediately to the desperate needs of displaced and trapped civilian populations within Bosnia.

GENOCIDE AND "ETHNIC CLEANSING"

The most striking aspect of the humanitarian side of the conflict in Bosnia and Herzegovina is that unlike most refugee flows, which are commonly a byproduct of war, the creation of civilian refugees in Bosnia is a major goal of the assault. Serb forces intentionally target civilians for killing, rape, detention, torture, and other abuses. Likewise, Serb militia actively encourage those who survive to flee their home areas. Some have been fortunate enough to gain access to bordering states and thus have become "refugees." Those unable to reach neighboring countries and those refused entry to such countries remain in the limbo of the internally displaced. In either case, one goal of the Serb militia is achieved: ethnic purity within regions they control. This is what has come to be known as "ethnic cleansing."

USCR staff have documented eye-witness testimony from Bosnians of actions that fit the definition of genocide in the Genocide Convention. These include: killing members of a particular group; causing serious bodily or mental harm to members of the group; and deliberately inflicting on the group conditions of life calculated to bring about its physical destruction in whole or in part. Such testimonies have also been gathered by human rights organizations such as Amnesty International and Helsinki Watch, as well as the UN Human Rights Commission and the U.S. government. Gross abuses of human rights and war crimes in the former Yugoslavia include murder, rape, detention, torture, and summary execution. The State Department's own human rights report for 1992 illustrates the horror:

Civilians were the primary targets of military action, making a mockery of the Geneva Conventions. Accompanying abuses of individuals and groups of non-Serbs took almost every conceivable form of torture, humiliation, and killing. The policy of driving out innocent civilians of a different ethnic or religious group from their homes, so-called ethnic cleansing, was practiced by Serbian forces in Bosnia on a scale that dwarfs anything seen in Europe since Nazi times.

HUMANITARIAN INTERVENTION

More than 800,000 Bosnians are internally displaced–forced from their homes, yet still trapped inside Bosnia. More than 100,000 have already died; and hundreds of thousands more could die. For many, survival depends on the assistance pipeline, which has operated, at best, in fits and starts.

UNICEF says that children in areas of heaviest attack are already showing signs of acute malnutrition, and that mothers frequently are eating half of what they need in order to make more food available for their children. Conditions are undoubtedly worse in isolated pockets that are completely cut off from contact with the outside world.

Although UN Security Council Resolution 770 calls for "all measures necessary" for humanitarian relief deliveries to reach needy populations in Bosnia, in fact, "all necessary measures" have not been taken. Lack of international support for its life-saving activities has placed the UN High Commissioner for Refugees (UNHCR) in the untenable position of having to beg and bribe Serbian extremists for permission to pass. This has not only seri-

RAPE CAMPS

Estimates vary widely, ranging from 10,000 to as many as 60,000. The most reasoned estimates place the number of victims at around 20,000.

The enormity of the suffering being inflicted on the civilian population in this conflict defies expression. Indications are that at least some of the rapes have been committed in particularly sadistic ways, so as to inflict maximum humiliation on the victims, on their family, and on the whole community. In many cases there seems little doubt that the intention is deliberately to make women pregnant and then to detain them until pregnancy is far enough advanced to make termination impossible, as an additional form of humiliation and constant reminder of the abuse done to them.

The Mission repeatedly heard accounts–including direct testimonies from a small number of victims–of multiple rapes against women in small centres (variously described as rape camps or "bordellos") located in schools, police stations, hotel restaurants, etc.

Excerpted from testimony by the European Council Investigative Mission before the Commission on Security and Cooperation in Europe, February 25, 1993.

ously compromised the authority of UNHCR in Bosnia, greatly complicating its mission, but also has directly impeded the delivery of life-sustaining goods, in direct violation of UNSC Res. 770.

FIRST ASYLUM

Of those who have escaped from Bosnia, many have found temporary refuge in other former Yugoslav republics. Of these, Croatia hosts the largest contingent, officially, some 324,000. However, the true burden on Croatia is even greater. With more than 250,000 Croatians still internally displaced as a result of earlier fighting in Croatia, the government of Croatia opted, in September 1992, to prevent any new Bosnian refugees from entering Croatia, saying it has reached its capacity, and citing inadequate offers by third countries to provide temporary asylum. With Crotia's borders effectively closed, Bosnians fleeing Serb attacks and deprivations were forced to remain–without the possibility of asylum or protection–within Bosnia, in bombed-out towns still under siege by Serb militia. To date, this remains the case.

Slovenia, which hosts about 50,000 refugees, has also closed its borders to new arrivals who do not have letters guaranteeing their acceptance by third countries. The Slovenian Ministry of Interior said that between 70 and 150 asylum seekers per day were being turned back.

When large numbers of refugees are forced to flee one country for the safety of another, it is an accepted international practice that the country to which the refugees flee–the country of "first asylum"–being the country most directly affected by the refugees' arrival, will have its burden shared financially and logistically by other countries outside the region. Croatia, for example, must spend approximately $2 million each day to care for refugees and displaced persons within its border. Until and unless the financial burden on Croatia is relieved through substantially increased financial assistance, it can be expected that Croatia will continue to prevent persecuted Bosnians from gaining entry to its territory. For many, this could mean that they will not survive the winter. Such a breakdown in the principle of first asylum not only guarantees an immediate humanitarian disaster, but increases the likelihood that similar breakdowns will occur in the future with frightening consequences for those trying to flee conflicts and persecution for years to come.

REFUGEE STATUS

In Croatia, Slovenia, Hungary, and other border states, Bosnian refugees have no firm legal status as refugees. In these and other European states, refugees are being treated on an ad hoc basis. They are vaguely defined as "externally displaced people" or as having "temporary refugee status," terms that are absent from the 1951 Refugee Convention or other international legal instruments relating to refugees. They are left in an uncertain legal position, needing to worry whether they will be permitted to work or travel or whether permission to stay will suddenly be withdrawn.

Refugees of special humanitarian concern for resettlement should include not only former civilian detainees, but also uprooted ethnically mixed families, and displaced female heads of households, particularly widows whose husbands have been killed as a result of the conflict.

WHAT IS EDITORIAL BIAS?

This activity may be used as an individualized study guide for students in libraries and resource centers or as a discussion catalyst in small group and classroom discussions.

The capacity to recognize an author's point of view is an essential reading skill. The skill to read with insight and understanding involves the ability to detect different kinds of opinions or **bias**. **Sex bias, race bias, ethnocentric bias, political bias,** and **religious bias** are five basic kinds of opinions expressed in editorials and all literature that attempts to persuade. They are briefly defined below.

Five Kinds of Editorial Opinion or Bias

SEX BIAS–The expression of dislike for and/or feeling of superiority over the opposite sex or a particular sexual minority

RACE BIAS–The expression of dislike for and/or feeling of superiority over a racial group

ETHNOCENTRIC BIAS–The expression of a belief that one's own group, race, religion, culture, or nation is superior. Ethnocentric persons judge others by their own standards and values.

POLITICAL BIAS–The expression of political opinions and attitudes about domestic or foreign affairs

RELIGIOUS BIAS–The expression of a religious belief or attitude

---

Guidelines

1. From the readings in Chapter One, locate five sentences that provide examples of editorial opinion or **bias.**

2. Write down each of the above sentences and determine what kind of bias each sentence represents. Is it **sex bias, race bias, ethnocentric bias, political bias** or **religious bias?**

3. Make up one-sentence statements that would be an example of each of the following: **sex bias, race bias, ethnocentric bias, political bias** and **religious bias.**

4. See if you can locate five sentences that are **factual** statements from the readings in Chapter One.

CHAPTER 2

UNIVERSAL HUMAN RIGHTS

10 UNIVERSAL HUMAN RIGHTS

HUMAN RIGHTS ARE UNIVERSAL

Warren Christopher

Warren Christopher is Secretary of State for the Clinton Administration. He made the following address at the World Conference on Human Rights in Vienna, Austria, on June 14, 1993.

Points to Consider:

1. How is the role of democracy defined?

2. What is the relationship between democracy and human rights?

3. How would a world of democracies be a safer world?

4. Evaluate the author's assertion that human rights are universal.

5. How are the prospects for human rights described?

American support for democracy is an enduring commitment.

I speak to you as the representative of a nation "conceived in liberty." America's identity as a nation derives from our dedication to the proposition "that all Men are created equal and endowed by their Creator with certain unalienable rights." Over the course of two centuries, Americans have found that advancing democratic values and human rights serves our deepest values as well as our practical interests.

That is why the United States stands with the men and women everywhere who are standing up for these principles. And that is why President Clinton has made reinforcing democracy and protecting human rights a pillar of our foreign policy–and a major focus of our foreign assistance programs.

DEMOCRACY

Democracy is the moral and strategic imperative for the 1990s. Democracy will build safeguards for human rights in every nation. Democracy is the best way to advance lasting peace and prosperity in the world.

The cause of freedom is a fundamental commitment for my country. It is also a matter of deep personal conviction for me. I am proud to have headed the U.S. Government's first interagency group on human rights under President Carter, who is with us today. President Carter will be remembered as the first American President to put human rights on the international agenda. He has helped to lift the lives of people in every part of the world. Today, we build upon his achievements–and those of the human rights movement since its inception.

In this post-Cold War era, we are at a new moment. Our agenda for freedom must embrace every prisoner of conscience, every victim of torture, every individual denied basic human rights. It must also encompass the democratic movements that have changed the political map of our globe.

I cannot predict the outcome of this Conference. But I can tell you this: The worldwide movement for democracy and human rights will prevail. My delegation will support the forces of freedom–of tolerance, of respect for the rights of the individual–not only in the next few weeks in Vienna, but every day in the con-

Cartoon by Mike Ramirez. Reprinted with permission: **Copley News Service.**

duct of our foreign policy throughout the world. The United States will never join those who would undermine the Universal Declaration and the movement toward democracy and human rights.

SECURING FREEDOM AFTER THE COLD WAR

The Universal Declaration enshrines a timeless truth for all people and all nations: "Respect for human rights and fundamental freedoms is the foundation of freedom, justice and peace" on this earth. The Declaration's drafters met the challenge of respecting the world's diversity, while reflecting values that are universal.

The promotion of democracy is the front line of global security. A world of democracies would be a safer world. Such a world would dedicate more to human development and less to human destruction. It would promote what all people have in common rather than what tears them apart. It would be a world of hope, not a world of despair.

Democratic aspirations are rising from Central Asia to Central America. No circumstances of birth, of culture, or of geography can limit the yearning of the human spirit and the right to live in freedom and dignity. Martin Luther King, Mohandas Gandhi, Fang Lizhi, Natan Sharansky–all came from different cultures and countries. Yet each shaped the destiny of his own nation and the world by insisting on the observance of the same universal rights.

UNIVERSAL RIGHTS

That each of us comes from different cultures absolves none of us from our obligation to comply with the Universal Declaration. Torture, rape, racism, anti-Semitism, arbitrary detention, ethnic cleansing, and politically motivated disappearances–none of these is tolerated by any faith, creed, or culture that respects humanity. Nor can they be justified by the demands of economic development or political expediency.

We respect the religious, social, and cultural characteristics that make each country unique. But we cannot let cultural relativism become the last refuge of repression. The universal principles of the UN Declaration put all people first. We reject any attempt by any state to relegate its citizens to a lesser standard of human dignity. There is no contradiction between the universal principles of the UN Declaration and the cultures that enrich our international community. The real chasm lies between the cynical excuses of oppressive regimes and the sincere aspirations of their people.

No nation can claim perfection–not the United States nor any other nation. In 1968, when the U.S. Delegation arrived at the first World Conference on Human Rights, my country was reeling from the assassination of Martin Luther King. The murder of Robert Kennedy soon followed. King and Kennedy were deeply committed to building a more just society for all Americans. Their valiant work and their violent deaths left deep imprints on an entire generation of Americans–among them, a university student named Bill Clinton.

NEXT STEPS OF OUR OWN

Beyond our support for multilateral efforts, the United States recognizes that we have a solemn duty to take steps of our own. In that spirit, I am pleased to announce that the United States will move promptly to obtain the consent of our Senate to ratify The International Convention on the Elimination of All Forms of Racial Discrimination. We strongly support the general goals of the other treaties that we have signed but not yet ratified. The Convention on the Elimination of All Forms of Discrimination Against Women; The American Convention on Human Rights; and The International Covenant on Economic, Social and Cultural Rights: All of these will constitute important advances, and our

CULTURAL RELATIVISM

Christopher's speech highlighted the issue of "cultural relativism," which is shaping up as one of the most controversial at the Conference as Western nations strive to defend the universality of human rights in the face of some Third World countries' demand for varying standards.

In preparation for this conference, 34 Arab and Asian governments issued the Bangkok Declaration, arguing that the notion of human rights is a relative one linked to the cultural, religious and historical diversity of nations. They demanded respect for national sovereignty and opposed using human rights "as an instrument of political pressures."

"Human Rights," **Washington Post**, June, 1993.

Administration will turn to them as soon as the Senate has acted on the racism Convention.

We will act to deter aggressors. And we will cooperate with like-minded nations to ensure the survival of freedom when it is threatened.

11 UNIVERSAL HUMAN RIGHTS

HUMAN RIGHTS ARE NOT UNIVERSAL

Jin Yongjian

The following is a statement made by Ambassador Jin Yongjian, head of the Chinese delegation, at the Fourth Session of the Preparatory Committee for the World Conference on Human Rights, April 21, 1993.

Points to Consider:

1. How is the Bangkok Declaration described?

2. What was China's role in the Bangkok Declaration?

3. How is poverty related to human rights?

4. Identify the different kinds of human rights.

5. Analyze the author's attitude toward universal human rights.

Excerpted from a speech by Jin Yongjian before the Fourth Session of the Preparatory Committee for the World Conference on Human Rights, April 21, 1993.

We should adopt a practical and realistic attitude, neither neglecting the protection of human rights nor putting this issue in an inappropriate scale.

As an Asian country, China participated in the Asian regional meeting held not long ago in Bangkok, Thailand and was elected as one of the vice-chairmen of the meeting. At that important gathering of countries of the Asian region, the overwhelming majority of Asian countries demonstrated the spirit of solidarity by having the cardinal principles in mind and taking the overall situation into account. They tried their best in seeking common ground while reserving differences, and reached a consensus. The Bangkok Declaration adopted at the meeting showed that Asian countries respect the principles and purposes of the UN Charter to safeguard and promote human rights and fundamental freedoms, and that they are determined to adopt practical measures to raise the level of human rights enjoyment by the Asian people. The basic spirit and contents of the Bangkok Declaration should be fully reflected in the final document of the World Conference.

FINAL DOCUMENT

In our view, the final document of the World Conference should:

1. Emphasize respect for the principles of national sovereignty, territorial integrity, non-interference in the internal affairs of states and the non-use of human rights as an instrument to apply political pressure; reiterate that all countries, large or small, have the right to determine their own political systems, to freely pursue their economic and social development; discourage any attempt to use human rights as a conditionality for extending development assistance; emphasize the principles of equality and mutual respect in conducting international human rights activities in order to strengthen international cooperation; and ensure a positive, balanced and non-confrontational approach and eliminate the practice of selectivity and double-standards in addressing and realizing all aspects of human rights.

2. Underline the essential need to create favorable conditions at both national and international levels for the effective enjoyment of human rights, bearing in mind the significance of national and regional particularities and various historical, cultural and

68

religious backgrounds, and viewing human rights in the context of a dynamic and evolving process of international norm-setting.

3. Reiterate the interdependence and indivisibility of economic, social, cultural, civil and political rights, and the need to give equal emphasis to all categories of human rights.

4. Strongly oppose massive, gross human rights violations caused by racial discrimination, racism, apartheid, colonialism, foreign aggression and occupation, as well as the recent resurgence of neo-Nazism, xenophobia and ethnic cleansing.

5. Reiterate, in light of the experience of the vast majority of developing countries that poverty is the main obstacle to the full enjoyment of human rights, that the right to development, as established in the Declaration on the Right to Development, is a universal and inalienable right and an integral part of fundamental human rights, which must be realized through international cooperation, and recognize that the main obstacle to the realization of the right to development lies at the international macroeconomic level.

6. Emphasize the importance of protecting the human rights and fundamental freedoms of vulnerable groups such as women, children, minorities, migrant workers, disabled persons, indigenous populations, refugees and displaced persons.

THE WORLD CONFERENCE

Today, 45 years after the adoption of the Universal Declaration of Human Rights, the convening of the World Conference on Human Rights will provide the international community with an opportunity to summarize experience and lessons from history, to carry forward the cause and forge ahead into the future. It will

enable us to set correct guiding principles for future international human rights activities. The event undoubtedly will have great significance. However, in preparing the final document for the conference, we have to take a realistic and objective attitude. The national conditions of different countries are extremely complex, and the international community faces many issues that cry for urgent solutions, such as international armed conflicts, social and political turmoils, profound racial contradictions, external economic environment, social prosperity and development, the arms race, population explosions, etc. They are all attracting universal attention and are calling for ways and means to deal with and resolve them. Human rights protection is one important link in the chain of our work, but it is not the whole of our work, nor can it replace our efforts in other areas.

So far as the UN is concerned, there are organs like the General Assembly, the Security Council and so on. They have their respective mandates in political, economic, social and other fields. The mandates and spheres of activities of these organs differ from one another. Only when each organ fulfills its own mandates can the United Nations perform its duty well. Therefore, we should adopt a practical and realistic attitude, neither neglecting the protection of human rights nor putting this issue in an inappropriate scale, thus affecting or even replacing the normal activities of other organs. To this end, the World Conference needs a balanced, fair and comprehensive final document. Only in this way can it be beneficial to the genuine and universal promotion and protection of human rights and fundamental freedoms. And only in this way can the World Conference make outstanding contributions to United Nations human rights activities and be carried into its history as such.

12   UNIVERSAL HUMAN RIGHTS

A COVENANT ON ECONOMIC RIGHTS: THE POINT

Donald Boudreaux and Karol Ceplo

Donald Boudreaux and Karol Ceplo wrote this article for the Ludwig von Mises Institute. The Institute is a conservative educational foundation located in Auburn, Alabama.

Points to Consider:

1. How do Americans think of rights and freedoms?

2. What does the United Nations mean when it uses the word "rights?"

3. Discuss the meaning of the "International Covenant on Economic, Social and Cultural Rights."

4. Why is the U.N. charter undemocratic?

5. Evaluate the reason given for the wealth of western nations.

When the United Nations uses the word "rights," it means entitlements, not liberties.

At the World Conference on Human Rights in Vienna, Secretary of State Warren Christopher announced U.S. support for a United Nations treaty declaring economic development as an inalienable right of all people. If the Senate goes along with the Clinton administration by approving this treaty, vast new sums of American wealth will pour into the coffers of foreign dictatorships.

RIGHTS

Americans generally think of rights as freedoms from government intrusion and oppression. Mention a "right to economic development" to a work-a-day American–generally speaking, any American not living off the government–and he will assume you are talking about the right to keep the fruits of your labor and be prosperous. He will not interpret this "right" as meaning an entitlement to prosperity.

But when the United Nations uses the word "rights," it means entitlements, not liberties. A "right" to economic development means that those lacking prosperity are entitled to the fruits of the labor of those who are prosperous. An entitlement implies the corresponding duty for someone to fund the entitlement. For example, last year, a Colombian delegate to the United Nations said the "right to development is the pillar for economic and social rights," yet "industrialized countries fail to recognize it."

A COVENANT

The treaty in question is the "International Covenant on Economic, Social, and Cultural Rights." It would impose unfair burdens on U.S. citizens. If citizens of Myanmar, Pakistan, or any other third-world country, have a right to be prosperous, Americans would be responsible not only for our own, but also the world's destitute. The obligation would last until poor countries attain some undefined minimum level of prosperity.

The views of Li Daoyo of China are representative: "If there is genuine concern about the human rights situation in developing countries, [industrialized nations should] provide those countries with unconditional assistance." Under this scheme, the Western taxpayer becomes a slave to the third world.

GOVERNMENTS

The U.N. charter is also grossly undemocratic. Enforcing these "rights" does not mean private investment, but rather money to governments. With lavish financing from developed nations, these governments will be free to tyrannize their peoples. They can maintain economic policies that help the powerful few at the great expense of the populace. Aid insulates governments from the needs and aspirations of their citizens.

These governments are like a monstrous teenager–that is, a teenager who believes he has an unlimited right to his parents' income and tolerance. If mom and dad buy him a new car every time he wrecks his current car, he will treat his car with carelessness. If his car develops a squeak or a knock signaling the need for repair, the teenager ignores it because he does not pay the price. Third-world governments on the U.S. dole treat their economies with equal disregard.

Also like spoiled teenagers, governments of underdeveloped countries will not wisely spend monies they receive as a matter of "right." They certainly won't promote free markets and pursue policies conducive to economic growth.

INCENTIVES

The treaty sets up perverse incentives. When the country's economy grows, the government lose its right to largess. Indeed, they themselves are obligated to contribute to the pot that funds countries still on the dole. Better, from the government's perspective, for the country to remain underdeveloped and dependent. Such moral hazards are an inescapable part of aid to poor countries.

Just as teenagers who enjoy virtually unlimited "rights" to their parents' wealth never really grow into responsible and self-sufficient adults, countries with a U.N.-backed "right" to development will never develop and prosper. Instead, they remain the ungrateful and whining wards of the U.N. The Clinton administration acquiesced to the U.N. position on economic rights to avoid what it called "a sterile debate." But it is the administration's and the U.N.'s position that is sterile.

74

POLITICAL VS. ECONOMIC RIGHTS

The enemies of human rights like to pretend that there are two kinds: "political rights" (free speech, worship, etc.) that the West emphasizes, and "economic and social and cultural rights" (the right to social and economic services guaranteed by the state) that non-Western countries champion. What's wrong with expanding the list of rights to include such nice things as the right to a guaranteed job...

What's wrong is that these rights intentionally undermine the very idea of political rights. A right is something that the individual claims against the state, a sphere of activity protected from state encroachment.

Economic rights are claims on the state by the individual to guarantee the necessities of life and thus are instruments for increasing state power over the individual.

Charles Krauthammer, **Washington Post**, June 26, 1992.

THE WEST

The West did not grow wealthy because some international organization declared prosperity to be a "right." It happened because countries relied upon free markets, limited their political institutions, and allowed entrepreneurial drive and creativity to do their work. The institutions necessary for sustained economic growth—self-denial, hard work, risk taking, and respect for the property of others—are undermined by wealth redistribution.

Free markets and capitalist institutions are the key to prosperity. The U.N.'s International Covenant on Economic, Social, and Cultural Rights will inevitably cause the wellspring of prosperity to run dry both at home and abroad.

13   UNIVERSAL HUMAN RIGHTS

A COVENANT ON ECONOMIC RIGHTS: THE COUNTERPOINT

Mari Marcel Thekaekara

Mari Marcel Thekaekara has spent the last ten years working with indigenous people in the hills of the Indian state of Tamil Nadu.

Points to Consider:

1. Who was responsible for the Bengal famine?

2. How does "structural adjustment" affect the poor?

3. How do the poor subsidize the rich in India?

4. What is the relationship between poverty and human rights?

5. Compare the way human rights are defined by Western countries and Third World nations.

Mari Marcel Thekaekara, "New World Ordure," **The New Internationalist**, June 1993. Reprinted with permission from **The New Internationalist**, June 1993. For further information contact **The New Internationalist**, 1101 Bloor St.W., Ste. 300, Toronto, ON Canada M6H 1M1.

Millions died begging for food in Bengal because Churchill's British Government diverted grain...

As a 16-year-old Calcutta schoolgirl, I wept for the Jewish people when I read Leon Uris's *Exodus*. Millions of people also died on the streets of Calcutta in 1943-44. But while Hitler's Holocaust is still vividly remembered, the Bengal Famine was and is barely mentioned–it was just an historical fact I tucked away in my mind for exams, even though millions of my own people had died so horrendously scarcely ten years before my birth.

MILLIONS DIED

Millions died begging for food in Bengal because Churchill's British Government diverted grain, making it impossible for any but the wealthy to buy what rice was left. These people were killed by Churchill's policies as surely as those Jewish Europeans were killed by Hitler's. What is it that makes the world agitate about one set of human rights and not another? Did the starving Bengalis not have as much right to live as the Nazis' hapless victims?

Who decides that a hue and cry must be made about one kind of atrocity while another gets away unpublicized? Who sets the agenda which sees imprisonment and torture as human-rights violations while torture and death by starvation are not? And what gives some countries the right to become "international" arbiters, ignoring the blood on their own hands?

The poor have never been a priority. Not now, not ever. History is in the process of repeating itself as the New World Order takes over. A new insidious form of colonialism is engulfing the world. It is more dangerous in its new manifestation. Earlier, the enemy was visible. Now the global takeover by powerful Western nations has the consent and active participation of legitimate, elected governments in Third World countries.

STRUCTURAL ADJUSTMENT

The World Bank and the International Monetary Fund (IMF) dictate the terms through the process of structural adjustment, the newest obscenity in the development dictionary. Open your markets, they decree. Cut public spending. Remove subsidies on health and food. (If people die in the process, population growth will be tamed; an added bonus.) Produce more goods for export.

Do all these things without fail or we will order sanctions against you.

India has just started down this road. We have opted for economic liberalization, privatization and free markets after four and a half decades of Nehruvian socialism–in spite of the disastrous results evident in Asian, African and Latin American countries. So we had, for the first time in our history, a Budget which openly and unashamedly pandered to the rich. Refrigerators, cars and colour TV sets became cheaper. But ration rice, the absolute basic necessity in India, became more expensive. The mainstream press hailed the Budget. It was lauded as bold, imaginative, innovative. Yet it pandered to just 3 per cent of the population while offering the remaining 97 per cent only desolation and despair.

A top-of-the-line colour TV had its price slashed by 2,500 rupees ($80) and advertisements now urge the rich to buy their second TV for the kids' bedroom. Meanwhile the price of a kilo of rice went up by 0.75 rupees, forcing the poorest to buy less rice for the family. An unskilled casual labourer in a tea estate here in the Nilgiris, for example, gets about 800 rupees ($25) a month and spends over 700 of this on food alone. The person who can afford a colour TV is likely to earn over 10,000 rupes ($320) a month and spend less than one-third of that on food.

INDIAN GOVERNMENT

So, proudly, even exultantly, the Indian Government has announced that in its new economic dispensation, the poor will have to subsidize the rich. But the poor are already feeling the effects of economic liberalization and structural adjustment. Here in the Nilgiris, Doctors Roopa and Deva, who have been running a community-health programme since 1987, are in despair because their growth-monitoring charts are showing children under five who had just made it out of malnutrition slipping back because their parents are buying less food. After five years of health education, of trying to get people to eat dal (the only protein available to the poor) the price of dal has become prohibitive. "We used to go to the shop and ask for a rupee worth of dal,"reports Kali, a tribal health worker. "But now the shopkeeper gets angry and tells us to get lost."

"Never mind dal," she continues. "Before we used to fill our stomachs with rice. Now you go to bed every night feeling hun-

FALLOUT FROM THE NEW GLOBAL ECONOMY!

Cartoon by Carol & Simpson.

gry, wishing you had just that little bit more which would give you the satisfaction of a full stomach." The indigenous people face a chronic protein deficiency anyway because their diet consists of bulk rice and little else. Now that they will have less rice as well, it will take its toll on their health, especially that of women and children.

We are already seeing children die because of poverty and malnutrition. Measles, diarrhea, a chest infection–minor ailments which a healthy child easily wards off-can wipe out the malnourished child. But will our government-accept moral responsibility for the deaths of these children as it slashes the price of TV sets and boosts that of rice? Or will the World Bank and the IMF who dictate the terms of structural adjustment own up to the blood on their hands?

Why are these starvation deaths not on the human-rights agenda? Why is there no pressure on the institutions which caused their deaths? Instead the West decides which are the "fundamental" human rights–and decides, for example, that individual freedom is what matters most, even if that means the freedom to exploit others.

TWO WORLDS

By the same logic, so long as there is a free world, children in the Third World will continue to starve to death so that their counterparts in the West can consume up to 20 times more resources "freely." And in the New World Order, coercion is permissible when it becomes necessary for the West to expand markets if it is to maintain its lifestyle.

There are signs of revolt, thank God. Amazingly, unexpectedly, farmers in India have been alerted to what the new General Agreement on Trade and Tariffs (GATT) agreement threatens to do to them. Under the agreement farmers would no longer have the right to replant their own seeds if these had been patented by multinationals. The plan is diabolical and would cripple our entire agricultural sector.

Farmers' unions throughout this vast country have managed to impress on their members the urgency of the situation. The godown (warehouse) and office of a major multinational was ransacked by demonstrators in Bangalore. Of course violence of this

80

sort by mere farmers will not be tolerated and the Government has threatened to take action. Only institutionalized violence is permissible.

The people will prevail. They always have, in the face of tremendous odds. But a bit of international pressure helps. It's time for people who care about human rights to adopt a new cause: the Third World person's right to exist. Our people are under fire from global terrorism of a terminal new order. Many have already been wiped off the face of the earth.

14   UNIVERSAL HUMAN RIGHTS

A COVENANT ON POLITICAL RIGHTS: POINTS AND COUNTERPOINTS

Carole Nagengast vs. Harold W. Andersen

Carole Nagengast made the following statement in her capacity as the National Chairperson of the Board of Amnesty International USA Harold W. Andersen follows her statement with a counterpoint he made as Chairman of the World Press Institute.

Points to Consider:

1. What is Amnesty International?

2. How does Carole Nagengast define the International Covenant on civil and political rights?

3. Why does she support this United Nations treaty?

4. How does Harold W. Anderson explain his opposition?

5. Why does he say this treaty violates the U.S. Constitution?

Excerpted from Congressional testimony given by Carole Nagengast and Harold W. Andersen before the Senate Foreign Relations Committee, November 1991.

CAROLE NAGENGAST - THE POINT

In recent years human rights has played a more central and significant role in U.S. foreign policy. But the United States is still far from accepting a single standard of human rights which it applies to all countries and which it applies domestically as well. U.S. ratification of human rights treaties will provide that solid base and single standard on which to appeal to all governments with respect to human rights abuses wherever they occur.

Amnesty International was established to promote human rights, to document and publicize violations of human rights and to work for victims of human rights violations around the world. We have long recognized the necessity of establishing an international legal framework for the protection of human rights. That has been done through the Universal Declaration of Human Rights and the international human rights treaties based on the principles of the Declaration. We look forward to working with this committee on a number of pending human rights treaties, including the Women's Convention, the Race Convention, the International Covenant on Economic, Social and Cultural Rights, and on the Children's Convention, as well as the treaty before us today, the International Covenant on Civil and Political Rights.

BASIC RIGHTS

The International Covenant on Civil and Political Rights protects fundamental rights including those at the core of Amnesty International's work: the right to be free from arbitrary killings, the right to freedom of conscience, expression and association, the right to be free from arbitrary arrest or detention, the right to freedom from torture and ill-treatment and the right to a fair trial.

We call on the U.S. Government to conform its record to its rhetoric. The "rule of law" applies to the United States as well as to other countries. The United States cannot be satisfied with pointing an accusing finger at other countries if it is not willing to have the light of accountability shine on itself as well. We call on the United States to contribute to solidifying the international framework for the protection and promotion of human rights by ratifying the International Covenant on Civil and Political Rights and cooperating in the international monitoring mechanisms it establishes. One of the most important implementing mechanisms of this treaty is contained in the First Optional Protocol to the treaty, which grants individuals a right of petition to the

Human Rights Committee. The United States ought to sign that Protocol and submit it to the Senate for its advice and consent.

WHY RATIFY THE INTERNATIONAL COVENANT ON CIVIL AND POLITICAL RIGHTS?

Ratification of the Covenant by an increasing number of states promotes the protection of international human rights in numerous ways. **First**, the Covenant is an agreement among nations setting rights and imposing obligations on states to protect those rights. The Covenant represents the consensus as to what is the meaning of human rights and gives added protection to individuals against violations of their civil and political rights. Further, it assures them that in the future each national administration will be subject to a continuing international obligation to guarantee specific and fundamental rights, no matter who is in power.

Second, ratification goes beyond merely recognizing and defining international human rights standards. Through ratification a nation agrees to standards against which its performance can be measured and monitored by its own citizens, by other nations and international organizations and by world public opinion. Acceptance by states of international obligations helps to establish a more durable commitment to the protection of human rights. It preserves important achievements by governments of today against retrogression by those of tomorrow.

Third, the Covenant strengthens the international machinery for the protection of human rights by providing a system of reporting and review of the Covenant whose provisions are based on and derived from the Universal Declaration of Human Rights. The Human Rights Committee was established in 1976 to oversee compliance with the Covenant on Civil and Political Rights and its Optional Protocol. It is a mechanism that not only provides a forum where human rights problems can be constructively addressed but also where incompatible or ill-founded allegations may be dispelled. Ratification will enable the United States to participate in the international human rights structures now open only to those states which have ratified the Covenant. Where human rights problems exist, adherence to a common framework of protection, mutually recognized among nations, can be a means of opening a constructive dialogue and identifying effective solutions. Furthermore, U.S. ratification of the Covenant will encourage other countries to ratify, and thereby further augment the effectiveness of the international human rights system.

Fourth, the credibility of the U.S. Government in promoting universal respect for human rights will be furthered by ratification of this Covenant. Unless a government has ratified the Covenant, it cannot credibly denounce other states for their violations of international standards which it has not itself accepted.

Fifth, as more nations ratify the Covenant, domestic advocates of human rights in countries that are persistent violators will be strengthened in protesting and combating those violations. The now historic example of Vaclav Havel in Czechoslovakia is one example that comes easily to mind. But there are many former human rights activists who are now in the legislatures or other government agencies in the former Soviet Union and Eastern European countries where repressive governments have recently undergone dramatic transformations.

Sixth, the Covenant legitimates concern and intercession by one country regarding the behavior of another government towards its citizens. This point is extremely important, for nations that violate human rights frequently hide behind convenient rationales of presumed interference in their internal affairs. Ratification of this treaty is an important indication that the United States is committed to the concept of human rights as a concern that transcends national boundaries. It strikes many U.S. citizens as odd that their government and that of the People's Republic of China are the only permanent members of the U.N. Security Council who are not parties to this treaty.

RATIFICATION

Amnesty International USA urges prompt ratification of the International Covenant on Civil and Political Rights. While its public rhetoric in support of human rights and the rule of law has increased in the last few years, the US Government has fallen seriously behind in advancing the practical application of the international rule of law, provided in the human rights treaties. It has not ratified many of the international human rights treaties.

The Convention on the Rights of the Child has not even been signed. It is time to match action to rhetoric. The ratification agenda of other pending human rights treaties is long, and there is much work that has to be done after it gives advice and consent to ratification of the Civil and Political Covenant.

HAROLD W. ANDERSEN - THE COUNTERPOINT

We believe that Articles 19 and 20 of the International Covenant on Civil and Political Rights not only threaten the freedom and independence of journalists and news media worldwide, but threaten also the individual citizen's right to freedom of expression–a right which the articles purport to protect. We do not believe that reservations or other accompanying statements will sufficiently lessen the problem. Our experience is that such reservations are ignored.

Article 19 starts by saying that everyone shall have the right to hold opinions without interference, and the right to freedom of expression, that this right shall include freedom to seek, receive and impart information and ideas of all kinds, regardless of frontiers, and through any media. But then Article 19 goes on to say: "The exercise of the rights provided for in...this article carries with it special duties and responsibilities. It may therefore be subject to certain restrictions, but these shall only be such as are provided by law and are necessary.

(a) For respect of the rights or reputations of others.

(b) For the protection of national security or of public order or of public health or morals.

Article 20, which follows next, states:

1. Any propaganda for war shall be prohibited by law.

2. Any advocacy of national, racial or religious hatred that constitutes incitement to discrimination, hostility or violence shall be prohibited by law.

Such invitations for restrictions can be used by governments to attempt to justify banning of news media and muzzling of individuals whose views the government finds offensive.

THE CONSTITUTION

In the Administration's original submission of the Covenant to the Committee in 1978, the Department of State said flatly that Article 20, "conflicts with the Constitution." Now you are being asked to approve the premise that other countries can reasonably accept provisions that we acknowledge would violate the Constitution here. We should set a better example.

These are the reservations which the Administration proposes. In regard to Article 19, the proposed declaration begins: "It is the view of the United States that states party to the Covenant should wherever possible refrain from imposing any restrictions or limitations on the exercise of the rights recognized and protected by the Covenant, even when such restrictions and limitations are permissible under the terms of the Covenant."

So the government of the United States endorses restrictions on individual and news media freedom whenever a foreign government finds it "not possible" to refrain from imposing restrictions. What a position to take in the eyes of the world!

NATIONAL SECURITY

The broad language in which both Articles describe possible restrictions–to "protect" national security or "public order," for instance–is sure to prove irresistibly tempting to some governments.

A few years ago South Africa sought to have journalists report only the news the government wanted. It proposed a code of conduct for journalists that was narrowly beaten back. This would have provided criminal penalties for violations which "affect the peace and good order of the Republic." South Africa's proposed code, incidentally, would have applied to foreign correspondents as well.

The authoritarian ruler of Kenya, President Daniel arap Moi, could live very nicely with the language of Articles 19 and 20. He could interpret it as, in effect, legitimizing the present ban on opposition political rallies challenging his one-party government, in the name of protecting public order.

A surprising new challenge to press freedom has developed in, of all places, the U.N. Human Rights Commission in Geneva. An important working paper, drawing its inspiration from these same Articles 19 and 20, focuses so heavily on what it calls "permissible limitations" on news that the main idea that the press should be free seems fogged over.

Can such problems be overcome by reservations or other ways while still ratifying this Covenant? Based on our experience, attempted qualifications as to these very articles are largely ignored. For example: The working paper at the U.N. Human

Rights Commission that I mentioned–the one outlining "permissible" restrictions–is a 67-page, single-spaced document. It dismisses in just two paragraphs the reservations to Article 19 taken by seven countries, and reservations taken to Article 20 by nine countries. If experts at a U.N. Human Rights Commission view treaty reservations this lightly, how are government officials striving to crush dissent likely to see them?

The Covenant was originally sent to the Senate in 1978 with the Secretary of State's comment that Article 20 was in conflict with the U.S. Constitution. It was not seen as fit for ratification for 13 years. We see no compelling reason to take it off the shelf now, especially in view of the danger that ratification, however qualified, could lend itself to restrictions on news, however unintended. To be worthy of a free society's support, such a Covenant should say that press and public should be free to write and speak without restriction–period. Anything less than that, unfortunately, poisons the entire document.

EXAMINING COUNTERPOINTS

This activity may be used as an individualized study guide for students in libraries and resource centers or as a discussion catalyst in small group and classroom discussions.

The Point
The Tibet question is an internal Chinese matter and should not be linked to U.S. trade policy.

The Counterpoint
The U.S. should restrict trade with China until the Chinese agree to withdraw from their brutal occupation of Tibet.

— • • • —

The Point
Human rights are universal.

The Counterpoint
Human rights are not universal because they are defined differently by different cultural and historical traditions.

— • • • —

The Point
The United Nations should have intervened militarily to prevent the genocide in Rwanda.

The Counterpoint
Military intervention is no way to deal with global violence and poverty.

Guidelines

Part A
Examine the preceding counterpoints and then consider the following questions.

1. Do you agree more with the point or counterpoint in each case? Why?

2. Which reading in this publication best supports the point in each case?

3. Which reading best clarifies each counterpoint?

4. Do any cartoons in this publication illustrate the meaning of the point or counterpoint arguments? Which ones and why?

CHAPTER 3

THE POLITICS OF TERROR

15   THE POLITICS OF TERROR

THE TRIUMPH OF WESTERN VALUES

George Roche

George Roche has served as president of Hillsdale College since 1971. He has appeared on "Firing Line," "The MacNeil-Lehrer News Hour," and "Today." His views have been chronicled in Newsweek, Time, Reader's Digest and the Wall Street Journal. He is the author of ten conservative books on political and social issues.

Points to Consider:

1. Describe the dismal performance of communism.

2. How does communism differ from capitalism?

3. According to Marx, how does capitalism cause poverty?

4. Why is capitalism ethical and efficient?

5. How have Western values triumphed over communism?

George Roche, "The Road to Freedom," **Imprimis**, Vol. 22, No. 7, July 1993. Reprinted with permission from **Imprimis**, the monthly journal of Hillsdale College.

Free men know what tyrants never learn, that the ultimate economic resource is the mind and energy of a free person.

The biggest story of our times is this: Communism is dying. But perhaps the most striking feature of its demise is that it is not accompanied by much of a celebration of the triumph of capitalism in the West. You would expect countless books, articles and spokesmen proclaiming victory for the free market. You would expect a massive intellectual defense and explanation of capitalist ideas–and perhaps some crowing about how much better they are. You also would expect political leaders in the West to redouble their efforts to expand liberty. True, there has been some of each of these, but there has been no concerted effort to claim victory.

The near-silence is ominous. It is as if we had achieved great ends with evil means and ought to be ashamed rather than exultant at our success. This guilty feeling is itself a communist hangover. We should be rid of it once and for all, or Marx will have the last laugh. Moreover, we must seek to understand the cause of the communist demise. Until we understand the cause, we will not be able to heal the frightful wounds communism leaves behind, and we will ourselves remain in peril of repeating the same mistakes.

DISMAL PERFORMANCE

We do know that without a doubt the economic performance of communism has been dismal everywhere it has been tried. Communism simply cannot compete with free markets. But it was not economic failure that really killed communism in Eastern Europe or the former Soviet Union or that is in the process of finishing it off in Latin America and Asia. We would be greatly mistaken if we assumed that people in closed societies only want more consumer goods. Certainly they would like more and better food, housing, clothes and appliances–wouldn't we all? But it is not a yearning for mere possessions that moves them. After all, they have from the beginning endured economic disaster and terrible privation.

Ultimately, the death of communism has been brought about by its own spiritual failure. The triumph of "capitalism" is equally a spiritual victory, but we in the West have been slow to recognize it as such. I put "capitalism" in quotation marks because it is a Marxist coinage and a hate word. It is also bad coinage–all systems are necessarily capitalist, because they all have to allocate capital. But everyone is pretty much agreed about its Marxist and principle meaning: a free market system based on the ownership of private property and the free exchange of goods. I am happy to accept this meaning and insofar as I use the term, that is what I mean by it.

SPIRITUAL DIMENSION

When I say capitalist ideas are better, I mean precisely in their spiritual dimension. Of course they are more efficient; everybody knows that. It is hardly worth saying. What few see, however, is their moral goodness...

According to Marx, the capitalist system alone causes poverty (by paying low wages), unemployment and periodic depressions. Private property is bad. Rent and interest are stolen from workers. Capitalists are all greedy, grasping, mean and exploitative...

It is little remembered now, but Marx first advertised his theories as more economically efficient. They got nowhere. In fact, they were drubbed by experience: Capitalism was booming and wages were rising rapidly when in the mid-19th century he published his predictions that workers would be reduced to poverty. Only when they lost the argument about efficiency did Marx and the communists turn to a moral argument, saying that capitalism was unjust. Only then did they prevail, for there was no rebuttal in moral terms. The claims of capitalist evils have been the whole strength of communism ever since and still pollute such intellectual swamps as Beijing, Ethiopia and a number of American college campuses.

MORALITY IN ECON 101

But capitalism is not unjust, nor is it unnatural or immoral; its structure and rules are as ethical as they are efficient. It is communism, on the other hand, that is unjust, unnatural and immoral, as is finally becoming clear after the cruelest century in human memory–a century when nearly 170 million people sacrificed their lives, mainly on the altar of statism and socialist or communist ideology. Whereas socialism and communism appeal to hatred and envy, capitalism not only appeals to our moral instinct to help others, but harnesses our energies to that purpose and

Cartoon by Richard Wright.

rewards most those who do the most for humanity.

All of us, you see, live in a whirl of activities that involves the transfer of goods and services. We sell our labor and produce, or rent and invest our capital, for money. With our money we buy food, clothing, shelter and the niceties of life. And there are only two ways goods can be transferred. The first is one-sided and involuntary to one of the parties...

The second kind of transfer is two-sided: Both parties voluntarily agree to the exchange. Its key feature is that it is freely chosen. This, and this only, may be called an economic exchange; the word exchange even implies mutual consent. When we see why both parties agree, we have the key to the whole of modern economic science. It is simply human nature...

A BRIGHTER ROAD AHEAD

There is a brighter road ahead, though, as evidenced by the fall of communism in Eastern Europe and the former Soviet Union. Against seemingly impossible odds, country after country has thrown off its communist yoke. In the Christmas season of 1989, we all watched a very special celebration in Berlin, and we knew the impossible dream had come true. East and West Berliners, reunited after decades, hugged, laughed, poured champagne, wept, and defiantly danced on that monument to barbarity that had divided them, the Berlin Wall. Uncounted millions wept and laughed with them, and church bells rang the world over. Here, for all humanity to see, was the symbolic reunion of long-divided Europe and of the world, in freedom.

Here, too, all saw that communism was no longer a potent idea contending for the minds and hearts of men. It was just one more instrument of power, naked power of men over men, such as we have seen countless times before in history. Its last pretensions as an idealistic moral philosophy collapsed as its borders were broken. The crimes it had so long concealed were laid bare; it lay in the destruction and reek of its own works, economically exhausted and spiritually destitute...

WHAT FREE MEN KNOW

For nearly a century, the Left in this country have claimed that socialism, whether represented by Soviet-style communism or European-style socialism, is morally superior to our market-based capitalist system. They have criticized every aspect of America, all the while chanting their chants and rattling their bones. They have compared our "failures," real and imagined, with their utopian pipe dreams.

Through the testimony of those forced to live under communism and socialism, we know that the truth is exactly the opposite of all the promises. In the former Soviet Union, in the name of "equality" and "economic justice," the party bosses gave themselves a cut of the wealth one hundred to one thousand times greater than that of the masses. They created a ruling class, the *nomenklatura*, more autocratic and exploitative than the tsars. In a system much like apartheid, except far more virulent, they reserved for themselves all the top jobs, the best education, the best medical care, and up to 100 percent of the quality goods sold in special stores that only they could patronize...

Free men know what tyrants never learn, that the ultimate economic resource is the mind and energy of a free person. Only from a free mind comes the direction of all productivity and the innovation that is tomorrow's prosperity. It is said that we now live in an information economy. This is true enough, but it is not the whole picture. Add to it an unprecedented mobility for the movement of economic resources–assets as well as data. Thought

96

and money can and do travel almost anywhere in a split second, too fast for the plodding state to catch up. It is this mobility and versatility that gives individuals the upper hand at last. There is no turning back.

THE GLOBAL MARKET

The growing power of the global marketplace is bringing this fact home everywhere. Its power has exposed the weaknesses of socialism and communism and has helped tear down the Iron Curtain. Its power is fundamentally moral and as such deserves all the moral support we can give it. The message of the post-communist newcomers to the marketplace is directed toward every would-be tyrant: "We are not things to be used by you, but free people with inalienable rights. In the market, it does not matter how we came into the world but what we make of ourselves. We join in cooperative effort for the good of all. If you interfere, you harm all people. If you oppress us, you will lose all that we have to offer and become poor. Throw away your chains and your barbed wire; they are useless now."

16   THE POLITICS OF TERROR

THE NEW WORLD DISORDER

Jack Nelson-Pallmeyer

Jack Nelson-Pallmeyer lived and worked in Central America for several years and is also the author of War Against the Poor: Low Intensity Conflict and Christian Faith *(Orbis Books, 1989) and* Brave New World Order: Must We Pledge Allegiance? *(Orbis Books, 1992.)*

Points to Consider:

1. Describe the three major economic trends that are shaking the foundations of the Old Order.

2. Why is winning the Cold War an ideological triumph rooted in lies and distortion?

3. What is the relationship of international hunger to the failure of capitalism?

4. How is domestic hunger and poverty in the U.S. described?

5. Compare the status of the rich and poor in the U.S.

Excerpt from **Brave New World Order: Must We Pledge Allegiance?** by Jack Nelson-Pallmeyer. © 1992 by Jack Nelson-Pallmeyer. Published by Orbis Books, Mary Knoll, New York 10545. Used by permission of the publisher.

A wall between the rich and the poor is being built, so that poverty does not annoy the powerful and the poor are obliged to die in the silence of history.

The *brave new world order* being fashioned by the United States is based on clearly defined roles. U.S. leaders are "predestined" to be world controllers. Poor people in and outside of the United States are being "conditioned" to accept their place as the equivalent of "future sewage workers" in Aldous Huxley's novel. Former President Bush has suggested that in the new world order the weak must learn to trust the mercy of the strong. Unfortunately, as we will see, the weak can expect neither mercy nor justice in the new order...

In addition to the obvious shift in the balance of military power in the post-Cold War period, there are three major economic trends that are shaking the foundations of the old order. Each involves a massive transfer of wealth:

• from poor nations to rich nations;

• from U.S. poor and working-class people, and from future generations, to U.S. elites; and

• from the United States to Japan and Western Europe...

However, these trends, deliberate and interrelated, are based on systematic exploitation. They are likely to foment considerable unrest both domestically and internationally...

A THIRD-WORLD PERSPECTIVE ON WHO "WON" THE COLD WAR

The nonviolent movements that swept through Eastern Europe and the rapid fall of the Soviet Union from superpower status surprised the world, but the process of disintegration had deep historical roots. Nonetheless, bureaucratic communist parties and the command economies they directed seemed to be discredited overnight.

Unfortunately, in the West the interpretation of these events was generally limited to self-congratulation rather than self-criticism. The Cold War was over, and we had won; we, of course, referred to the United States, the West, and capitalism. Democracy and the international market system had triumphed.

"Winning" the Cold War, for the United States, is an ideological triumph rooted in lies, distortions, and historical blindness. It is possible to proclaim victory because the failures of the Soviet-dominated order are real and obvious and because important facts are suppressed.

For example, one of four U.S. children is born into poverty. This statistic symbolically illustrates a deeper crisis: As the Cold War ended, the United States was the lone global military super-power, but the weakest economic partner in a tri-polar world dominated by Japan and Western Europe. The dynamics of this crisis, and its relation to the new world order, are the subject of the following section.

If claims of victory in the Cold War are dubious in light of child-hood poverty and U.S. economic decline, then they are also questionable from the perspective of Third World peoples whose countries are allied with the "victorious" Western powers. Pablo Richard, a liberation theologian working in Costa Rica, writes:

"The world changed abruptly in the last months of 1989...But has the life and death situation of the poor and oppressed masses of the Third World really changed? The Berlin Wall fell, and the rich world trembled with joy. In reality, the fall of the wall was very positive. But we are aware that another gigantic wall is being constructed in the Third World, to hide the reality of the poor majorities. A wall between the rich and the poor is being built, so that poverty does not annoy the powerful and the poor are obliged to die in the silence of history. A wall of silence is being built so that the rich world forgets the Third World. A wall of disinformation...is being built to casually pervert the reality of the Third World."

In addition to the reality of childhood poverty within the "victorious" United States is the fact that the majority of the approximately 40 million people who die each year from hunger live in Third World nations dominated by the United States and its Western allies. The victims of hunger and poverty are not primarily casualties of the Soviet Empire. They are victims of the international market economy which is being heralded as the savior of Eastern Europe and all of humanity...

POOR NATIONS

Jon Sobrino, a Jesuit priest from El Salvador, speaks of the self-

AUTH © **The Philadelphia Enquirer.** Reprinted with permission of UNIVERSAL PRESS SYNDICATE. All rights reserved.

deception of the First World or Western countries as a scandalous coverup. Shortly after the murder of two women and six priests at the hands of U.S.-trained soldiers in El Salvador he wrote:

"Wealth and power cannot exist if other people do not die, if people do not suffer in powerlessness and poverty and without dignity...We say that the First World, the wealthy countries, cover up the greatest scandal in this world, which is the world itself. The existence of two-thirds of humankind dying in poverty is covered up."

The poor majorities living in Latin America, the Caribbean, the Philippines, and many other Third World countries find little comfort in hearing that the Cold War is over and "we" won. Their countries have been integrated into the international market economy for generations, and they are living in nations with close political, economic, and military ties to the United States. Presumably, they are on the winning side of the Cold War conflict. However, their lives are condemned to poverty, inequality, and oppression.

The contradiction should be obvious. We rightly equate food shortages and long lines in the Soviet Union with failures of communism, but we fail to see domestic and international hunger in light of the failure of capitalism and the international market economy. The United States celebrates democratic movements and social changes in Eastern Europe. However, it blocks the possibility of similar changes within the U.S. sphere of influence...

RICH NATIONS

"The forces of the late twentieth century have required double-entry bookkeeping: new wealth in profusion for the bright, the bold, the educated and the politically favored; economic carnage among the less fortunate. In short, the United States of the 1980s."

–Kevin Phillips, *The Politics of Rich and Poor*

Poor people living in Third World countries are not the only victims of the so-called new world order. At the heart of this "new" order is a troubling paradox: Poor people within the United States, and the country as a whole, are getting poorer at the same as the rich within the United States are getting richer.

The massive wealth drain from Third World countries to First World elites has not prevented the economic decline of the United States. Its pressing national problems mirror those of many Third World countries.

The infant mortality rate in inner-cities like Detroit and Washington, DC, exceeds that of impoverished Honduras. The United States, in less than two decades, went from being the world's largest creditor nation to being the world's largest debtor. It is also a country of stark contrasts including billionaires and homeless people, measles epidemics and military bands, crack babies and Wall Street speculators.

The most disturbing parallel between the United States and the Third World is that massive wealth transfers from the Third World poor to the First World rich have a domestic counterpart. During the 1980s there was a dramatic shift in wealth from poor and working-class Americans to U.S. elites. This upward redistribution of wealth was accompanied by a radical shift in relative wealth and economic power from the United States to Japan and Western Europe. There is one other paradox that is central to understanding U.S. goals within the new world order: *The nation's declining economic power is accompanied by and linked to United States ascendancy as the world's undisputed leader in military power.*

DOMESTIC HUNGER AND POVERTY

The Reagan and Bush years produced, according to Kevin
Phillips, a Republican party strategist, "one of U.S. history's most
striking concentrations of wealth." This wealth concentration
occurred "as the American dream was beginning to crumble not
just in inner-city ghettos and farm townships but in blue collar
centers and even middle-class suburbs."

The gap between the richest and poorest U.S. citizens is now
greater than at any time since the Census Bureau began collecting
such data in 1947. The poorest 20 percent of the U.S. population
receive 3.8 percent of national income; the richest 20 percent get
46.1 percent.

If talk of victory in the Cold War sounded bitterly ironic to poor
people living in Third World countries allied with the United
States, it is doubly so for people living in Third World conditions
within the United States. The following litany of ills provides
ample evidence of a nation in crisis:

- One in four children in the United States is born into poverty;

- More than 35 million U.S. citizens lack any type of health
  insurance. Millions more have only limited coverage.

- The United States ranks 22nd in infant mortality, behind most
  of our industrial allies.

- Most of the poor in the United States are full-time workers or
  their dependents. This reflects a serious deterioration in the
  wages and benefits of significant sectors of the U.S. work
  force.

- In 1985, 20.4 percent of all infants below age 1 were not fully vaccinated against polio, 41.5 percent of infants of color.

- One-fourth of the poorest low-income households spend more than 75 percent of their incomes for rent.

- The United States has the world's largest per capita prison population. 426 of every 100,000 people are in jail. By way of comparison, the incarceration rates per 100,000 people are 333 in South Africa, 268 in the Soviet Union, 97 in Great Britain, 76 in Spain, and 40 in the Netherlands.

- The United States, according to a United Nations Development Program report, also has the highest murder rate and highest incidence of reported rape among industrialized countries.

These acute social problems are a consequence of national policies and priorities that enrich certain sectors at the expense of others. These policies include enormous tax cuts for the richest Americans, major cuts in social services, huge trade and budget deficits, and massive infusions of foreign capital. They reward speculative rather than productive investment and emphasize military production and power over socially useful production.

U.S. policies border on economic apartheid as U.S. elites, like their Third World counterparts, impose austerity measures on the poor. Most graphically, as economic opportunities and federally funded housing units are severely limited by budget cuts, the poor find "alternative housing" in prisons...

THE END

The end of the Cold War also offered hope for the United States, where economic problems were well advanced but not terminal. Judicious use of hundreds of billions of dollars of savings from the long-awaited "peace dividend" coupled with major tax, economic, and social reforms, offered possibilities for hope and revitalization. The world was standing at the threshold of a new world order.

Unfortunately, the possibility of an authentically new order threatened entrenched interests and was quickly dashed. The possibility of meaningful reforms lay dead in the sand, a premeditated casualty of the Gulf War. It was replaced with a "brave new world order" that suited elite U.S. interests.

17   THE POLITICS OF TERROR

INDONESIA AND AMERICA: PARTNERS IN GENOCIDE

Allan Nairn

Allan Nairn is a journalist who wrote the following article based on an assignment for the New Yorker Magazine. *He witnessed and survived a massacre at the Santa Cruz cemetery in East Timor. His article described a cold-blooded execution when Indonesian soldiers opened fire on a peaceful, defenseless crowd.*

Points to Consider:

1. How is the massacre in East Timor depicted?

2. Describe the terror of life in East Timor.

3. How is the U.S. implicated in the human rights violation by Indonesia in East Timor?

4. How should U.S. policy change toward Indonesia?

Excerpted from Congressional testimony by Allan Nairn before the Senate Foreign Relations Committee, February 27 and March 6, 1992.

The question now is whether the Congress will choose to support the continuation of mass murder with U.S. arms.

This massacre was only the latest mass atrocity in what has been one of the greatest genocides of the 20th Century. Two hundred thousand people, one-third of the East Timorese, have been murdered by the Indonesian troops. They have been executed in school yards, machine-gunned in open fields, and snatched from their homes and dropped into the sea. Some have died while fleeing through the rocky hills pursued by planes and helicopters. Others have succumbed to starvation and disease while confined to prison camps and resettlement villages. When I first visited East Timor in August of 1990, Timorese would furtively approach me almost whenever I went outside and ask me to get messages to the outside world. They would usually start by saying that the army would kill them if we were caught, for in East Timor, they explained, "it is prohibited to speak to foreigners." They would say "they killed my father," "my mother," "my brothers," "my wife," and run through the urgent litany of how the army had murdered their loved ones. People handed me notes and letters and pleaded that I tell their story to the U.N. Secretary General, the Parliament of Portugal, the Prime Minister of Australia or the Congress of the United States.

I have spent a dozen years covering armies and repressive regimes in places like Central America, Southern Africa and the Middle East, but I have never seen a place where the authorities have succeeded in making so many people so terrified. Downtown Dili is dotted with army torture houses and there are troops and plain-clothes agents everywhere. In the country, police descend on any outsider who enters a village, and they keep track of who is in each hut at night. I spoke with Indonesian troops and intelligence men who confirmed that they had killed 200,000. Several thousand of these were Timorese who resisted Indonesia with arms after its army invaded there in 1975. But the vast majority were simply civilian Timorese who either lived in towns that the army had chosen to destroy, or who had expressed opposition to Indonesian army rule or were unlucky enough to be children of people who had.

THE FUNERAL

When I returned to East Timor in 1992, the air of terror was

106

It's true that many of our Free World Allies regularly torture political prisoners.

But we shouldn't be overly concerned.

Our Western Civilisation demands certain sacrifices.

No pain ... No political gain.

Kirkpatrick

Carol & Simpson 1984

Cartoon by Carol & Simpson.

more intense and the repression was greater still. Sebastiao Gomes' funeral was a breakthrough event because people turned out and dared to speak. Some held up their hands in the sign of the "V" and shouted "Viva East Timor." The commemorative procession was even larger and more outspoken. As the mass broke up people assembled on the street. The army intelligence chief drove by. Along the route of march there were soldiers and police who carefully eyed the passing Timorese. This time a number of people were carrying hand-lettered banners supporting the church and the cause of Timorese independence. The banners said things like "Indonesia, Why You Shoot Our Church?" One was a plea addressed to "President Busch." There were young men, young women, children in Catholic school uniforms, and old people in traditional Timorese dress.

As the procession wound through Dili, many other people joined; they came from schools and offices and huts along the road. Sometimes young boys would break into a jog and older men would reign them in shouting "Disciplina!" "Disciplina!" People were chanting and giving the "V" sign and talking among themselves. By the time it reached the cemetery, the crowd had grown quite large. There were perhaps 3,000 to 5,000 people. Some filed in toward Sebastiao's grave, and many others remained outside, hemmed in on the street by cemetery walls. People were, at that point, standing around, talking excitedly among themselves, when, suddenly, someone noticed that one of the exit routes had been sealed off by an Indonesian troop truck.

Then, looking to our right we saw, coming down the road, a long, slowly marching column of uniformed troops. They were dressed in dark brown, moving in disciplined formation, and they held M-16's before them as they marched. As the column kept advancing, seemingly without end, people gasped and began to shuffle back. I went with Amy Goodman of WBAI/Pacifica radio and stood on the corner between the soldiers and the Timorese. We thought that if the Indonesian force saw that foreigners were there, they would hold back and not attack the crowd.

THE KILLING

But as we stood there watching as the soldiers marched into our face, the inconceivable thing began to happen. The soldiers rounded the corner, never breaking stride, raised their rifles and fired in unison into the crowd.

Timorese were backpedaling, gasping, trying to flee, but in seconds they were cut down by the hail of fire. People fell, stunned and shivering, bleeding in the road, and the Indonesian soldiers kept on shooting. I saw the soldiers aiming and shooting people in the back, leaping bodies to hunt down those who were still standing. They executed schoolgirls, young men, old Timorese, the street was wet with blood and the bodies were everywhere.

As the soldiers were doing this they were beating me and Amy; they took our cameras and our tape recorders and grabbed Amy by the hair and punched and kicked her in the face and in the stomach. When I put my body over her, they focused on my head. They fractured my skull with the butts of their M-16's.

The soldiers put us on the pavement and trained the rifles at our heads. They were shouting "Politik! Politik!" We were shouting back, "America! America!," and I think that may have been the thing that saved us. They had taken my passport earlier, but Amy showed them hers, and the soldiers seemed impressed when they realized that we were indeed from the States. We were, after all, citizens of the country that supplied them with M-16's. For whatever reason, the soldiers chose to let us live. We hopped a passing truck and got away. The soldiers were still firing as we left the scene, some 5 to 10 minutes after the massacre began.

This was, purely and simply, a deliberate mass murder, a massacre of unarmed, defenseless people. There was no provocation, no stones were thrown, the crowd was quiet and shrinking back as the shooting began. There was no confrontation, no hothead who got out of hand. This was not an ambiguous situation that somehow spiralled out of control. The soldiers simply marched up in a disciplined, controlled way and began to fire massively on the crowd.

It was quite evident from the way the soldiers behaved that they had marched up with orders to commit a massacre. They never issued a warning; they did not even pause or break their stride: they marched up and opened fire in unison. This action was not the result of their interaction with the crowd: the Timorese were just standing there or trying to get away. The soldiers opened fire as soon as their column turned the corner and got within a dozen yards of the Timorese.

U.S. ROLE

This formulation, however, understates the U.S. role. By continuing to provide arms shipments, training, and commercial arms sales to an army that massacres civilians, the U.S. government is itself an accomplice to an unmistakable, heinous crime. The Pentagon and CIA also share intelligence with Indonesia, and, from the U.S. embassy in Jakarta, the U.S. military attaches and the military group advise the Indonesian military on the use of U.S. equipment and provide military instruction and advice. This is all in addition to direct U.S. economic aid, yearly U.S. financing channeled through the Export-Import Bank and the U.S. contributions to the IGGI (Inter-Governmental Group on Indonesia).

One Pentagon official I spoke to said that it was his prediction that the Congress would respond to the massacre merely by cutting the $1.8 million in IMET aid. He said that this would be a way of making a public statement while at the same time avoiding unduly upsetting the Indonesians. He said that if the IMET aid were cut, Indonesia would understand. It would continue to take its U.S. weapons deliveries. And, likewise, he said that U.S. arms contractors would have no reason to complain. Arms manufacturers I spoke to on this subject echoed the confidence of the Pentagon man. They did not think there was any danger that Congress would interrupt the weapons flow.

THE CONGRESS

But if the Congress agrees with this course, the significance will be clear. The United States will be telling and showing Indonesia that they can stage a public massacre, watch deliberately as the wounded die, then kill witnesses and prosecute survivors, persecute priests, lie to the world–and have their generals declare that it is policy–and then be answered by fresh deliveries of American weaponry and money. This would be a crime, both in the legal and the moral sense. The United States would be knowingly arming an illegal occupation by an army with a policy of killing those who speak. The United States has done this from the beginning, since President Ford and Henry Kissinger met with Suharto in Jakarta 1 1/2 days before the invasion of Dili. The United States responded to the subsequent massacre by doubling Jakarta's military aid. The question now is whether the Congress will choose to stand up and enforce the law, or whether, in lieu of self-determination and free elections for East Timor, it will choose instead to support the continuation of mass murder with U.S. arms.

18   THE POLITICS OF TERROR

PROMOTING GLOBAL SECURITY IN ASIA

Kenneth M. Quinn

Kenneth M. Quinn wrote the following article in his capacity as acting Assistant Secretary for East Asian and Pacific Affairs in the Bush Administration.

Points to Consider:

1. How is the massacre in East Timor portrayed?

2. What action has the Indonesian government taken in regard to the killing in Dili, East Timor?

3. Describe the history and status of East Timor.

4. Why should East Timor be part of Indonesia?

5. How will the U.S. deal with Indonesia?

Excerpted from Congressional testimony by Kenneth M. Quinn before the Senate Committee on Foreign Relations, February 27 and March 6, 1992.

Indonesia considers that its takeover of East Timor was forced on it by the threat of a Marxist insurgency.

We are here today principally out of concern over the tragic event in Dili, when Indonesian army and police units fired on unarmed civilians engaged in a political demonstration, killing and wounding scores of people. The U.S. government has long been concerned about the human rights situation in East Timor. Officers from our Embassy in Jakarta have gone there frequently over the years.

The United States has publicly condemned the Dili incident. No provocation could have warranted such a wanton military reaction; the excessive use of force was unjustified and reprehensible. We immediately called for a complete and credible investigation leading to appropriate punishments for those who resorted to or condoned such deadly use of force. We clearly conveyed our views at high levels in both Jakarta and Washington. The issues now requiring U.S. policy judgments are these: how can the United States best help to ensure that our goals of accountability and a just resolution of the incident are realized, and that the well-being of the people of East Timor is improved?

We have been encouraged by the fact that the Indonesian government has also characterized the incident as a tragedy. Senior leaders are well aware that the world is watching. They understand that their positive international reputation, of which they are proud, is on the line. Our hope and expectation has been that Indonesia would move vigorously to find the facts, assess responsibility, appropriately punish those responsible, and take steps to prevent such an event from occurring again.

EAST TIMOR: HISTORY AND STATUS

The underlying issue in the incident is the status of East Timor, a Christian enclave of 750,000. After the 1974 leftist coup in Portugal, Lisbon decided to rapidly decolonize its overseas empire. This resulted in widespread chaos, civil conflict and foreign intervention in Portugal's former colonies. Angola and Mozambique endured 17 years of Marxist rule and brutal civil war that has only recently ended.

East Timor could have suffered a similar fate. When the new Portuguese government in 1974 decided to decolonize, East Timor was completely unprepared for self-governance. Four cen-

EAST TIMOR KILLINGS

The government of the Republic of Indonesia deeply regrets that an incident occurred that caused casualties among civilians. In response, a National Commission of Inquiry was established by the President of the Republic of Indonesia to investigate the matter thoroughly. The commission has found the total number dead to be 50 people. The officers who were involved in the incident have been tried, and those convicted have been punished in accordance with Indonesian law. This incident was clearly not reflective of the policies of the government of the Republic of Indonesia in East Timor.

Suhaswoto Hidyoningrat, **Wisconsin State Journal**, October 14, 1992. Hidyoningrat is consul for Information, Social and Cultural Affairs for the Republic of Indonesia in Chicago.

turies of colonialism had left East Timor with one high school, fewer than 10 college graduates, and a literacy rate under 10 percent. Portugal and Indonesia held discussions about the colony's future, but a civil war erupted there before any agreement was reached. The combatants were: Fretilin, which sought immediate creation of an independent Marxist state; another group that advocated immediate integration into Indonesia; and a third, which preferred a gradual decolonization process.

Portugal's leftist government abruptly withdrew in August 1975, handing over to Fretilin weapons which were then used to gain the upper hand. In the face of a Fretilin military victory and the declaration of an independent Marxist state, Indonesia invaded in December of 1975–and indicated it did so at the request of the East Timorese factions opposed to Fretilin. When the world turned its attention to East Timor in the mid-1970s, self-determination was not a realistic option. The choice was Marxist rule by Fretilin or action by Indonesia. Neither had a mandate from the ballot box.

It is important to recall that, since President Suharto rose to power in the mid-1960s, Indonesia has not had an expansionist agenda; East Timor is the only addition to what was once Dutch colonial territory. Indonesia considers that its takeover of East Timor was forced on it by the threat of a Marxist insurgency. The political context here is significant: The annexation of East Timor

113

occurred amidst active communist insurgences in much of Southeast Asia as the United States departed from Vietnam, and with memories of an attempted 1965 communist takeover in Indonesia still fresh.

UNIFICATION

Even before independence, Indonesian leaders had begun weaving that unifying fabric. They chose Malay, a minor trading language, rather than majority Javanese to be the national language. They promoted religious freedom for Christian, Hindu, and Buddhist populations scattered throughout the archipelago, despite a Muslim majority. To this day, Indonesian leaders strongly resist any advocacy of an Islamic state. A number of radical Muslims have been prosecuted over the years for promoting such a course. Indonesia's leaders have stressed unity because of their nation's immense diversity. They continue to insist on it today.

In 1976, U.S. policy-makers decided to accept Indonesia's incorporation of East Timor as an accomplished fact. They judged that nothing the United States or the world was prepared to do could change that fact. Thus, to oppose Indonesia's incorporation would have had little impact on the situation. With such reality in mind, previous administrations fashioned a policy which has been followed consistently on a bipartisan basis.

We accept Indonesia's incorporation of East Timor, without maintaining that a valid act of self-determination has taken place. Clearly, a democratic process of self-determination would have been more consistent with our values; but the realities of 1975 did not include that alternative. Accepting the absorption of East Timor into Indonesia was the only realistic option.

Since then, we have maintained a constructive dialogue with the Indonesian government designed to promote the well-being of the people of East Timor. Included in this has been an on-going human rights dialogue. That dialogue is generally private and is conducted at high levels; it is those characteristics that have made it effective.

THE DIALOGUE

Politically, we support discussions between Indonesia and Portugal under the auspices of the U.N. Secretary General as were mandated by the U.N. General Assembly in 1982. We believe such a dialogue continues to be the most promising avenue for resolving the East Timor issue. We are pleased that such a dialogue between Indonesia and Portugal at the U.N. Human Rights Commission meetings, which just concluded in Geneva, led to a constructive and balanced Chairman's Statement concerning human rights in East Timor.

Economically, our constructive relationship with Indonesia has allowed us to extend assistance to all Indonesians, which especially benefits the East Timorese. On a per capita basis, we have provided more than twice as many A.I.D. project dollars to East Timor since 1988 as to the rest of Indonesia.

Additionally, Indonesia has, on a per capita basis, funneled over six times as much of its own economic development budget into East Timor as to any other province. In 1991, East Timor received about $170 million in Indonesian Government grants. The $170 million, one might note, is, in nominal terms, almost exactly 100 times the average yearly development expenditure for East Timor in the last days of colonial rule, all of which was in the form of repayable loans.

The results of such recent investment are striking:

- In 1974, after four centuries of colonial rule, East Timor had 47 elementary schools, 2 middle schools, 1 high school, and no colleges. Now it has 574 elementary schools, 99 middle schools, 14 high schools, and 3 colleges.

- In 1974, East Timor had 2 hospitals and 14 health clinics. Now it has 10 hospitals and 197 village health centers.

- In 1974, East Timor had 100 churches. Today it has 518.

- In 1974, East Timor had 20 kilometers of surfaced roads, all within Dili. Now it has 428 kilometers throughout the province.

- In 1974, East Timor was plagued with endemic poverty. Today, poverty remains a problem, as it does elsewhere in that part of Indonesia, but starvation is extremely rare.

The missing economic element is sufficient employment to fulfill rising expectations of newly educated youth. But new business investors insist on a peaceful environment. And that remains problematic until the East Timor issue is fully resolved.

115

CONCLUSION

In conclusion, let me reiterate our major policies for dealing with the situation in East Timor:

(1) We intend to work cooperatively with the Indonesian Government to promote development and respect for human rights in the province; and

(2) We support the 1982 U.N. decision to promote an Indonesian-Portuguese dialogue under the auspices of the U.N. Secretary General to resolve the East Timor issue.

19   THE POLITICS OF TERROR

U.S. PARTICIPATION IN TORTURE AND TERROR

Penny Lernoux

Penny Lernoux, now deceased, was the Latin American Affairs Writer for the National Catholic Reporter *when she wrote the following article.*

Points to Consider:

1. Describe the message in the book *Torture in Brazil*.

2. What did President Raul Alfonsín do about the fate of thousands of disappeared in Argentina?

3. How did the U.S. promote tyranny in Brazil?

4. How did the U.S. encourage torture in Brazil?

5. What role did the C.I.A. play?

6. Discuss the extent of torture, terror and killing in Brazil.

Penny Lernoux, "CIA Syllabus in Torture Class," **National Catholic Reporter**, August 12, 1988. Reprinted with permission, **National Catholic Reporter**, Kansas City, MO.

One of the most disturbing aspects of Torture in Brazil *is its account of U.S. participation in Brazil's institutionalization of torture.*

One evening, recalls the Cardinal of São Paulo, a military judge came to his home to talk about his work in the Brazilian courts. An apparently cold-blooded individual, the judge admitted to Dom Paulo Evaristo Arns that he was upset about a murder case. Two different individuals had confessed to killing the same person at different times in totally different circumstances. Their confessions, said the judge, had obviously been extracted under such severe torture that "they were willing to declare themselves murderers even though they were not."

TORTURE

Cardinal Arns' chilling anecdote opens *Torture in Brazil*. The book provides detailed documentation of the horrors that went on in that Portuguese-speaking nation between 1964, when the military seized power, and 1979, which marked the beginning of the end of the dictatorship.

While many are aware of the brutalities committed by Argentina's last military regime because of the publicity surrounding the ongoing trial of nine former junta members, similar events in Brazil have been largely ignored. Repression continued over such a long period that it apparently ceased to be newsworthy. Fear was also an important factor in the silence: Only since a democratically elected government took power in 1985 have the Brazilians begun to speak publicly of the recent past.

RAUL ALFONSÍN

One of the first acts of Argentine President Raul Alfonsín following his election in late 1983 was to appoint a commission to investigate the fate of the thousands of disappeared. The result was an explosive document, *Never Again*, based on the testimony of the relatives of the disappeared and political prisoners who had survived the concentration camps. The commission's work was dangerous because even after Alfonsín became president, paramilitary groups continued to kidnap and torture critics of the previous regime. But the situation of the 30 religious people, lawyers and former political prisoners responsible for the Brazilian project was still more precarious because the military remained in power throughout their investigations.

Protected by Arns and financed by the World Council of Churches, the investigators worked under the name of an innocuous-sounding São Paulo institution, Testimonies Pro-Peace (TPP). The secrecy was necessary not only to safeguard their lives, but also to obtain nearly one million pages of government documents, mostly court cases, before the military could destroy such incriminating evidence. Unlike Argentina's *Never Again*, which was questioned because it depended on unofficial testimony, the documentation in the Brazilian version is based on the government's own records and is therefore irrefutable.

For Brazilians, the work provides a memory of events that should not be forgotten, in order that they may not occur again. For Americans, it offers yet another lesson on the terrible consequences of U.S. intervention in Latin America.

AMERICAN INFLUENCE

As documented in the archives of the Lyndon B. Johnson Library, Washington strongly encouraged the 1964 coup that led to more than two decades of dictatorship in Brazil. The reasons were familiar: The elected civilian government was mildly reformist and had challenged the power of U.S. multinationals.

Of the 7,367 arrests studied by the TPP team, most occurred immediately after the coup and in the late 1960s and early 1970s when Washington was extolling the Brazilian "economic miracle" as a model for other developing nations. Although the miracle proved to be a brief mirage, leaving Brazil the most indebted nation in the Third World, for its duration foreign corporations made huge profits on the backs of a captive labor force that was literally beaten into submission by the military. Unions and strikes were outlawed, and labor leaders who spoke out against the erosion in real wages were hauled off to government torture centers.

One of the most disturbing aspects of *Torture in Brazil* is its account of U.S. participation in Brazil's institutionalization of torture. Military court documents show that torture classes were part of the police and military training curricula; political prisoners served as guinea pigs. Among those to introduce such "pragmatism" were CIA agents, who taught the Brazilians how to administer pain without killing the prisoner, as, for example, in the application of electric shock. U.S. congressional hearings of the period reveal that U.S. embassy officials were aware of the widespread use of torture but ignored it because of the military government's warm reception of U.S. investment.

THE REPRESSION

Although repression was legalized through a series of draconian decrees, military and police death squads usually did not bother with legal niceties. In 84 percent of the cases studied by the TPP, the prisoners were held incommunicado, unable to speak with their families or a lawyer, in countervention of the military's own laws.

The scope of the repression is suggested by the number of witnesses involved in the more than 7,000 cases. More than 10,000 people were drawn into the military's web because they happened to know the accused. Most were arrested and tortured although they were not charged with any crime.

While the Argentine military regime popularized the tactic of "disappearing" political prisoners, the Brazilians were the first in Latin America to use torture scientifically in order to cow the population. Testimony shows that, when arrested, many prisoners were prepared to admit to anything, even murder, to avoid the horrors of the torture chambers–to no avail, because were always tortured.

120

Methods ranged from the "parrot's perch," in which the prisoner was hung upside down and beaten or subjected to electric shocks, to the "dragon chair," a device invented in the Rio de Janeiro military police barracks whereby the prisoner received electric shocks while a dentist's drill shattered his or her teeth. Male prisoners were then held upside down while their testicles were crushed.

Among the most fiendish inventions was the "icebox," a tiny freezing cell connected to ear-splitting loudspeakers designed to drive the prisoner crazy. Animals were also used in torture sessions, including snakes and cockroaches, the latter forced into the anus.

No one was immune. Pregnant women were raped and so severely tortured that they aborted. Children were also tortured or forced to watch their parents mistreated. Although students and workers comprised the largest number of victims, opposition politicians, journalists and priests and nuns were also singled out for repression.

TRAGEDY

The tragic story of the Dominican friar Tito de Alencar Lima illustrates the lasting marks left by torture. Arrested in São Paulo in 1970, the priest suffered such terrible atrocities that he tried to kill himself in prison. Later released and exiled to France, Frei Tito hung himself in 1974.

In his suicide note written in a São Paulo prison, Frei Tito said he had decided to take his life to publicize what was happening and to prevent others from suffering the same fate. Americans, too, may learn from *Torture in Brazil*, because the U.S. government played a major role in bringing the Brazilian military to power in 1964.

20   THE POLITICS OF TERROR

AN AMERICAN COMMITMENT TO DEMOCRACY

Warren Christopher

Warren Christopher made the following speech as Secretary of State in the Clinton Administration. He spoke at an Organization of American States luncheon in Washington, D.C.

Points to Consider:

1. How has the U.S. promoted democracy in the hemisphere?

2. What are the two greatest challenges in the hemisphere?

3. Describe the role NAFTA plays between North America and nations of the hemisphere.

4. What is meant by nations of the hemisphere?

Excerpted from a speech by Secretary of State Warren Christopher, Washington D.C., March 26, 1994.

We must make progress on the two greatest challenges in our hemisphere–strengthening democracies and sustaining economic reform.

Foreign ministers, heads of delegation, Mr. Secretary General: I appreciate your joining me in our continuing dialogue within this hemisphere. I would like to recognize our Commerce Secretary, Ron Brown. I also want to recognize my Deputy Secretary, Strobe Talbott, who will lead the U.S. delegation at the Organization of American States (OAS) meeting tomorrow. Let me also note the presence of Sol Linowitz, former U.S. Representative to the OAS, negotiator of the Panama Canal Treaties, and one of the great figures in hemispheric relations.

As we come together today, the Americas share a deep sorrow over the tragic assassination of Mexican Presidential Candidate Colosio. We extend our sympathies to the people of that nation, and we reaffirm as a hemisphere our collective commitment to uphold democracy and oppose violence. Luis Donaldo Colosio represented hope for his country. His death is a great loss for his nation and for our hemisphere, but I believe Mexico will find renewal in its people and in the new generation of leaders so well represented by President Salinas.

DEMOCRACY

In that respect, I might note that we are gathered in a room named for Thomas Jefferson, perhaps our nation's greatest proponent of democracy and constitutionalism. Once, looking back at the election of 1800, Jefferson commented that historic change in America's leadership was "not affected by the sword, but by the rational and peaceable instrument of reform, the suffrage of the people." Our democratic institutions and the values our nations uphold have been tested by violence many times since. But I am confident they will pass this tragic test, as they have passed others.

We all owe a great deal to Secretary General Baena Soares for his leadership over the last 10 years. The election of a new OAS Secretary General is an ideal opportunity to renew and reinforce our common efforts. The agenda of the next Secretary General will be full–promoting democracy and human rights, expanding trade and investment, strengthening hemispheric security, combatting narcotics, and widening technical cooperation. In each of these areas, the OAS has an important and growing role to play.

123

In the Americas, as in other parts of the world, regional challenges require effective and creative regional organizations.

ORGANIZATION OF AMERICAN STATES (OAS)

When the nations of this hemisphere meet in the OAS, each has one vote–no matter the size of that nation's population, territory, or economy. We respect each other's sovereignty, and we recognize the rights and needs of all our members. The United States is working through the OAS on the many important problems that elude bilateral solutions. The unanimous approval of the Washington and Managua Protocols by the U.S. Senate Foreign Relations Committee is a sign of our commitment to the OAS. These protocols, which we anticipate the full Senate will approve for ratification shortly, represent important progress in our collective defense of democracy and in our commitment to balanced development.

We must make progress on the two greatest challenges in our hemisphere–strengthening democracies and sustaining economic reform. The Mexican Presidential election will send a vital signal throughout the hemisphere. It will signal that we are committed to strengthening multilateral diplomacy–to deepening and expanding the cooperation among us. It will enable the OAS to build upon its recent successes and to command maximum respect and resources for the future. We must ensure that the powerful movement to democratic governments and open markets in this hemisphere becomes irreversible. We must grasp the historic opportunity to expand trade and investment and promote sustainable development.

NAFTA

The United States, Mexico, and Canada took a decisive and constructive step by ratifying the North American Free Trade Agreement (NAFTA). We expect NAFTA to be a platform for greater prosperity within North America and a bridge to greater economic integration throughout the hemisphere. We hope the Summit of the Americas in Miami will produce initiatives that accelerate this momentum. The United States is also developing measures that address concerns about the effect of NAFTA on trade and investment in the Caribbean Basin countries. This effort was set in motion by President Clinton after he met with Caribbean leaders and with Central American leaders.

DEMOCRACY

For nearly six decades, the observance of the annual Pan American Day has told the world that the nations of the Western Hemisphere share a unique harmony of ideals–the love of liberty, independence, and democracy; the willingness to seek these treasures and to preserve them wherever they are found; and firm and profound opposition to totalitarianism. Each year the United States joins with countries throughout the Americas in pledging fidelity to these ideals so vital to our future.

President Ronald Reagan, Pan American Day Proclamation, April 11, 1988.

Our intention is to extend to the Caribbean Basin obligations and benefits similar to those under NAFTA. We hope to achieve greater liberalization in the textile and apparel sector and greater protection for investment and intellectual property rights.

CONCLUSION

We need to consult carefully and thoroughly with Congress before going forward. I can assure you that the nations of the Americas have before them a period of great promise and great hope. Looking at the Summit of the Americas, President Clinton has said that "we have a unique opportunity to build a community of free nations, diverse in culture and history, but bound together by a commitment to responsive and free government, vibrant civil societies, open economies, and rising living standards."

The OAS has a chance to shape this brighter future. I look forward to working with each of you to ensure the success of our collective effort to build a more open and more prosperous hemisphere.

21   THE POLITICS OF TERROR

SUPPORTING TERROR
IN EL SALVADOR

National Catholic Reporter

National Catholic Reporter *is an independent Catholic newsweekly based in Kansas City, Missouri.*

Points to Consider:

1. According to the reading, what role did the U.S. play in the civil war in El Salvador?

2. What does the UN's Truth Commission report unearth about the twelve-year civil war?

3. What were some of the atrocities committed during the war?

4. How was U.S. policy toward El Salvador throughout the 1980s justified? Should U.S. policy toward El Salvador change?

Credit: "Salvador Nightmare Demands Further Reckoning," **National Catholic Reporter**, March 23, 1993. Reprinted with permission, **National Catholic Reporter**, Kansas City, MO.

U.S. policy in El Salvador was little short of criminal.

In November 1989, during the Farabundo Marti National Liberation Front offensive, San Salvador was crawling with so many journalists that there were seldom enough taxis to go around. Reporters and photographers often rode toward the fighting crammed four to a cab, with only a flapping white flag and the letters TV taped to the windshield between them and El Salvador's murderous civil war.

Yet, deep in the curfew hours of Nov. 16, as if to spit in the eye of that international scrutiny, U.S.-trained government troops invaded the Centroamericana University campus, hauled Jesuit Father Ignacio Ellacuría with seven of his colleagues and companions from their beds and executed them. Maybe the only thing more audacious than that deadly raid was the belief of those who ordered it that they could get away with it.

TRUTH COMMISSION

With publication of the United Nation's Truth Commission report on some of the atrocities of Salvador's 12-year civil war, that audacity is easier to understand, even for some who remained unconvinced that U.S. policy in El Salvador was little short of criminal.

The report confirmed what many had long known. Government forces under various guises killed and maimed at times indiscriminately, on a scale nearly ten times greater than that of the rebels, and members of the military high command ordered the murder of the Jesuits.

Do it without leaving witnesses, said then-Col. Rene Emilio Ponce, whom U.S. officials later backed to become defense minister. Trouble is, the world was a witness, and this time the human rights hounds did not let up. Groups in and out of El Salvador, the Jesuits prominent among them, insisted on justice. Salvador's corrupt judicial system finally jailed a scapegoat colonel for the murders, but critics knew that was hardly a hem of the whole cloth.

U.S. POLICY

In the United States, mainline support for continued aid to El Salvador began to erode. The Salvador military had apparently hoped that killing the Jesuits would extinguish the rebel's intellec-

Cartoon by Carol & Simpson.

tual light, but what flared from the muzzles of those M-16's that November night helped illuminate an international process that eventually led to the January 1992 peace accord, leaving the government far short of a military victory. To ice the irony, the peace accord established the U.N. commission that unearthed the evidence so damaging to the military's version of the war. Truth was coming to light like bones from the mass grave at El Mozote, in the area where the army massacred about 800 civilians, most of them women and children, in 1981.

The cover-up following that massacre, in Salvador and in the United States, pinned down the pattern for the decade, the same pattern of disinformation and deceit that allowed Ponce and others to believe that they could get away with butchering the Jesuits. The two journalists who reported what they saw in El Mozote were discredited as rebel dupes, partly through U.S. State Department testimony before Congress. But for the next decade it was really the American people who were duped.

DENIALS

Time and again, U.S. officials stepped forward to deny or explain away Salvadoran government crimes and cover-ups while assuring Congress and the people that military aid should continue because the human rights situation in El Salvador was improving.

128

Remember, for example, Alexander Haig, Reagan's Secretary of State at the time, suggesting the four U.S. religious women raped and murdered outside San Salvador in 1980 may have been involved in "an exchange of fire" with the Salvador National Guard. Or Haig's colleague at the United Nations, Jeanne Kirkpatrick, implying the women were "political activists" and may have gotten what they deserved for sticking their noses into another nation's business.

But the United States was sticking its nose into that nation's business to the tune of $6 billion in military aid alone, all in the name of defending democracy from a communist takeover of Central America. That was a chimera, as many believed at the time and subsequent world events demonstrated.

Ponce resigned as defense minister a few days before the U.N. report was issued, apparently to head off political embarrassment and U.S. aid cuts for President Alfredo Cristiani's government. Cristiani, after scrambling to delay publication of the report, was quick to urge amnesty for all crimes the Truth Commission cited, amnesty in the name of national reconciliation. His argument was specious. No true reconciliation can be founded on the perpetuation of injustice and lies. Forgiveness is one thing, amnesty another. Forgiveness does not preclude punishment.

EL SALVADOR

Their villages have been bombed, their homes and crops burned, their friends, relatives and children harassed, tortured, killed. Yet the faith of the people–and their hope for a political solution–remain strong...

There is over 50-percent unemployment in El Salvador. There are half a million displaced Salvadorans in the country. The average daily wage is three colones–fifty cents a day. A bottle of Coca-Cola costs one colón, one-third of a day's wages. Those people who have work are really working as slaves.

Rev. John R. Quinn, "Notes on My Visit to El Salvador," **America**, May 3, 1986.

RESPONSIBILITY

Those responsible for the war crimes must be called to account, or there will be no national healing in El Salvador. At least 75,000 war dead, many thousands of them civilians, cry out for even that simplest sense of justice.

To their credit, rebel Marti National Liberation Front (FMLN) leaders rejected Cristiani's call for amnesty and urged full implementation of the U.N. recommendations, including penalties against some of their own. The commission documented several hundred civilian deaths at the hands of the FMLN, but it appears the rebels almost never killed indiscriminately. They were not, in other words, making war on the people they were trying to liberate, or "save for democracy."

The United States, as one of the primary perpetrators of injustice in this affair, should be pushing hard to set it right, for the sake of its own soul, if nothing else. Yet, Reagan/Bush henchmen, such as former Assistant Secretary of State Elliot Abrams, a right-wing ideologue and consummate liar, were calling the commission report a rewriting of history and insisting that U.S. involvement in El Salvador was a noble fight for democracy. That is the "democracy" that had the late right-wing thug Roberto D'Aubuisson running for president years after most of the world knew he was behind the assassination of Archbishop Oscar Romero. The commission report confirms the D'Aubuisson-death squad connection.

MURDER AND TERROR

U.S. economic and security assistance to this culturally diverse country–$75 million in 1989, $60 million in 1990–flowed. More than 200 U.S. companies had operations there... Guatemala citizens lived under Central America's most murderous government. In 30 years, its military, secret police and usual collection of hired gunmen killed an estimated 100,000 people, forced 150,000 into exile and internally displaced more than 1 million.

Colman McCarthy, **The Washington Post**, November 3, 1992.

PEACE

Perhaps no country deserves peace and a measure of normality more than El Salvador. But the U.N. report makes clear that before it will happen, there is work to be done and lessons to be learned. The United States has to be a part of that process. We cannot call others to account without being accountable ourselves. No doubt Abrams and his ilk knew that. But we should not let their deceptions divide us, or the people of El Salvador, any longer.

22 THE POLITICS OF TERROR

BUILDING DEMOCRACY IN EL SALVADOR

Panel on El Salvador

The following article was taken from a U.S. Secretary of State's report which was the result of a three-month comprehensive assessment of how the Department of State and the Foreign Service handled human rights issues, including El Salvador, from 1980 to 1991.

Points to Consider:

1. Compare the criticisms of U.S. human rights policy in El Salvador by Americans on the political left and right.

2. How is U.S. policy toward El Salvador defined?

3. Why was human rights an important factor in U.S. policy toward El Salvador?

4. How did the U.S. pressure the Salvadoran government to improve their human rights record?

5. In what ways has the situation in El Salvador improved?

Excerpted from a report of the U.S. Secretary of State's Panel on El Salvador, July 1993.

"There was no way to sustain our policy toward El Salvador without an aggressive approach on human rights. It was essential morally and politically."

Role of Human Rights in U.S. El Salvador Policy: Much of the criticism of the State Department and the Embassy over the decade derived from an argument whether human rights or prosecution of the war should be the overriding goal of U.S. policy. Critics on the left contended that the Department was willing to overlook human rights abuses by the Salvadoran military in pursuit of success in the war. Critics on the right argued that policies to promote human rights and democratic institutions were weakening the forces the U.S. Government needed for support in the fight against Communism. The State Department's attempt to pursue both goals at the same time satisfied no one at either end of the spectrum. Disputes also focused on the Administration's emphasis on the election process and institution building as ways to secure long-term protection of the human rights of Salvadoran citizens.

HUMAN RIGHTS

Strong underlying forces ensured that the promotion of human rights would be a critical element of U.S. policy toward El Salvador despite the changes in rhetoric. First, there was an assumption in the State Department that the Salvadoran government and society had to reform and develop a friendly, stable government supported by its people or there would be no hope to avoid an rebel Marti National Liberation Front (FMLN) takeover. Without reform, military aid would be wasted. Second, without improvements in the barbaric human rights practices in El Salvador, support in the United States for aid to that government would collapse. Pressures from Congress, the American public, and interests groups made progress on human rights issues key to continued U.S. assistance. Third, the Foreign Service reflects the nation it serves: human rights are an integral part of what we stand for as a nation and by the 1980s had become an accepted part of the American diplomatic agenda. Fourth, there were legal requirements to prepare the annual Human Rights reports, certifications of Salvadoran human rights performance, etc. As one former Assistant Secretary summed it up for the Panel: "There was no way to sustain our policy toward El Salvador without an aggressive approach on human rights. It was essential morally and politically."

Pressuring the Salvadoran Government on Human Rights: The files contain reports of sustained efforts by U.S. ambassadors in San Salvador and other members of the Administration to pressure the Salvadoran government and military to improve their record on human rights throughout the period. There is nothing in the record to suggest official indifference on this issue. U.S. ambassadors in San Salvador pressed their message firmly throughout the period that U.S. support for El Salvador was unsustainable if the human rights violations continued. Most did so publicly, as well as in private. The techniques applied included trips to the country by Vice Presidents Bush and Quayle and visits by many senior Washington officials, statements by U.S. leaders to Salvadoran visitors, numerous general and specific calls by U.S. ambassadors, and continuing efforts by members of the Embassy to get results on specific cases of human rights abuses. The most dramatically successful of these efforts was the trip by Vice President Bush in December 1983. His message to assembled officials and military leaders was blunt: stop the death squads or the President and I will lead the charge in stopping aid to El Salvador. His entourage provided a list of leading military figures who had to be moved out of command positions if U.S. aid were to continue.

VIOLENCE

Over the decade, however, the situation clearly improved. Some of the worst offenders were weeded out of the security services. By the mid-eighties, there was a sharp drop in the incidence of right-wing violence. At the same time, left-wing urban violence came to the fore with the killing of the Marines, the attacks on mayors, and the kidnapping of President Duarte's daughter in September 1985. Some critics of U.S. policy argue that the improvement was illusory, and that the tactics of the security services merely became more sophisticated as they found ways short of murder to continue their repression. Most observers agree, however, that the trend was certainly toward improvement until the 1988 murder of ten prisoners at San Sebastian by a military unit and the killing of the six Jesuit priests in the Pastoral Center of Central American University by government forces in November 1989. The latter widely-publicized incident reminded the world in dramatic terms that the Salvadoran "culture of violence" had not ended.

Critics of Administration policy argued that the only way to end rightist abuse was to stop giving American aid to the military. Some asserted that to give such aid to authorities who abuse human rights is to be complicit in their actions. Others felt that at least a convincing threat of an aid cut-off might have helped. But the Administration was generally unwilling to halt or threaten the military assistance which was seen as necessary to successful conclusion of the war. Only once was it temporarily curtailed: to force progress in the Jesuit case. Administration spokesmen contended that the situation in El Salvador was more likely to improve if the United States stayed engaged than if we abandoned the military completely. Furthermore, they argued that the situation would be far worse if the FMLN took over. Congress regularly voted for military assistance, though sometimes at reduced levels.

THE DEBATE

There were also prolonged arguments over whether ranking Salvadoran military leaders were directly involved in human rights abuses. American opponents of U.S. policy tended to see the military and security forces as a tightly-knit group in which top military leaders either ordered or at least tolerated continuing abuses by their underlings and death squads. The Department and the Embassy knew this might be true in specific cases and no one disputed there had been cover-ups. But the U.S. Government could not accuse, and attempt to have removed, individuals unless it had facts to support their case. Some people interviewed by the Panel argued that the U.S. Government did not have the luxury of

135

making accusations based on presumption or unconfirmed reports, particularly since it had to deal with military leaders on other matters.

Outsiders tended to see the Embassy as possessing enormous power, whereas those inside were acutely aware of the limits of that power, particularly when it came to changing long-standing patterns of violence. And Embassy personnel had no real option but to work with Salvadoran counterparts to reform the military, the police, and other organizations as well as to help fight the war.

INSTITUTION BUILDING

The State Department and the Embassy felt that the best approach to managing the Salvadoran problem was to build a civil society with appropriate institutions that could develop links between the government and the people and provide the basis for progress in human rights and other areas. Current and former officials whom the Panel interviewed held that Salvadoran society in the early eighties had become so polarized that the only hope for the country's future stability was to build a political center. The military had been running the country for a long time and had contempt–sometimes justified–for the corruption of the civilian governmental structure. The constraints on the civilian leadership's power were readily observable.

The Embassy, therefore, worked closely with Presidents Duarte, Magana, and Cristiani to devise ways to increase the power of civilian authorities in the country and encouraged military leaders to accede to this change. It strongly supported elections to pull political forces from the extremes to the center and give the winners the legitimacy necessary to govern. It sought to professionalize the army and inculcate more humane values in its ranks. The U.S. Government also worked hard to create an improved security and judicial system. The judiciary, however, was badly intimidated and shied away from any action on controversial cases.

The U.S. made a conscious decision to work through existing organizations both to increase their experience and prestige and to ensure the reforms had a "made in El Salvador" tag so they would last. As Assistant Secretary Enders told a Senate Foreign Relations Committee in early 1982, the Department believed that, though the judicial system was "very largely inoperative," the investigation of prominent cases had to be carried out within the

Salvadoran system if it were ever to begin fulfilling its proper functions. He added that, "We are asking them not only for justice, we are asking them to make the judicial system work, because it is an essential ingredient of human rights in any country."

Commenting on the slow process of institution building, one officer noted that by the time of the Jesuit murders in 1989, there had been real progress, with the Salvadoran security people moving from using torture as their most common investigatory tool in 1980 to modern, American-style investigation techniques. But it was hard to publicly demonstrate any real progress when the court system always seemed to look for ways to let people off. Another officer noted that even in the sophisticated U.S. court system it takes several years for reforms to take hold. To expect overnight changes in the non-functional Salvadoran judiciary was simply to expect too much.

Some see this effort to build Salvadoran institutions through the eighties as a major success which provided the confidence and process that allowed for the possibility of reconciliation in the nineties. A succession of U.S. ambassadors and State Department officials understood this approach to be a key goal of U.S. policy in El Salvador throughout the eighties.

23 THE POLITICS OF TERROR

A SCHOOL FOR KILLERS

Vicky A. Imerman

Vicky A. Imerman wrote this article in her capacity as the co-director of the School of the Americas Watch. SOA Watch was established in 1991 to counteract the lack of information available to the general public on the U.S. Army School of the Americans and its role in U.S. military policy in Latin America.

Points to Consider:

1. What is the School of the Americas?

2. Describe the meaning of low-intensity conflict.

3. Analyze the relationship between low-intensity conflict and the School of the Americas core curriculum.

4. How does the School of the Americas teach and practice propaganda?

5. Why should the School of the Americas be closed?

Vicky A. Imerman, "SOA—School of Assassins," **CovertAction Quarterly**, Fall 1993. This article was adapted from **CovertAction Quarterly**, Fall 1993, number 46, 1500 Massachusetts Avenue #732, Washington, DC 20005, (202) 331-9763. Annual subscriptions in the U.S. are $22; Canada $27; Europe $33. The issue **CovertAction Quarterly**, containing the full text of the article with footnotes is available from CAQ for $8 in the U.S. and $12 other.

"If [SOA] held an alumni association meeting, it would bring together some of the most unsavory thugs in the hemisphere."

On March 15, 1993, the United Nations Truth Commission released its Report on El Salvador and cited over 60 Salvadoran officers for ordering, executing, and concealing the major atrocities of ten years of civil war. At least 75 percent of the censured officers trained at the U.S. Army School of the Americas (SOA) during their military careers. School commandant José Alvarez denied the involvement of SOA graduates in war crimes and called critics "ignorant" and "uninformed."

One of this nation's most secretive schools, SOA was established in Panama in 1946 to promote regional stability and train U.S. soldiers in jungle warfare. It evolved to teach low-intensity conflict, psychological operations, and intelligence gathering to some of the worst dictators, war criminals, and violators of human rights in the hemisphere. In their heydays of military abuse, Bolivia in the '60s, Nicaragua (under the Somozas) in the '70s, and El Salvador in the '80s were all primary clients of the SOA.

As the notoriety of its alumni grew, the school earned the nickname "Escuela de Golpes," or "School of Coups." In 1984, when Panama finally ousted SOA (under a provision of the Panama Canal treaty), the Panamanian daily *La Prensa* added another nom de guerre: "The School of Assassins."

Four years after relocation to Fort Benning, Georgia, SOA established a "Hall of Fame" to honor distinguished alumni. Honorees were flown from Latin America for award ceremonies attended by local VIPs, military brass, and occasional Congress members. "If [SOA] held an alumni association meeting," said Rep. Martin Meehan (D-Mass.), "it would bring together some of the most unsavory thugs in the hemisphere"...

LOW-INTENSITY CONFLICT

The core of SOA's curriculum, Low-Intensity Conflict (LIC), is a deliberately misnamed warfare strategy designed to maintain U.S. military influence in this hemisphere without using (or losing) large numbers of U.S. troops. Instead, U.S. military personnel, aided by a handful of guest instructors from various SOA client nations, train surrogate Latin American and Caribbean soldiers in "dirty little war" techniques, including: counterinsurgency and

urban counterinsurgency; irregular warfare and commando operations; sniper and sapper techniques; combat arms and special operations; and military intelligence. SOA graduates who go home and adequately perform their duties can look forward to returning to the SOA again and again, to receive more training, more free vacations to Disneyland, an assignment as guest instructor, or induction into the SOA Hall of Fame.

In this way, SOA functions not only as a training and indoctrination center, but also as a reward to select soldiers for a job well done. The perk street runs both ways according to Joseph Blair, a U.S. Army officer who taught logistics at SOA from 1986 to 1989. "American faculty members readily accepted all forms of military dictatorship in Latin America and frequently conversed about future personal opportunities to visit their new 'friends' when they ascended to military or dictatorial power some day."

The implications extend beyond the personal. Like any elite school, SOA builds an "old boys" network. When it comes time for the U.S. to choose one or another faction in an internal power dispute abroad, it has highly-placed allies whose politics it helped shape and whose loyalty it claims.

THE SMILING FACE OF OPPRESSION

SOA not only teaches the craft of propaganda, it practices it. SOA's rigorously promoted programs such as "Nation-Building" and "Internal Defense and Development" paint a benign facade on training here at home and U.S. military activities abroad. The short-term, public agenda of these "internal defense and development" projects includes bridge-building and medical aid tasks. Their long-term effect–like that of LIC as a whole–is to expand the bounds of military authority, to entrench the military in traditionally civilian areas, and to incorporate military propaganda and intelligence networks throughout civilian society.

While trainees absorb highly sophisticated propaganda and psychological operations techniques, they are initiated into the U.S. political line. In a course on "The Church in Latin America" (not listed in SOA course catalogs), trainees learn that Liberation Theology is a subversive doctrine promoted by the allies or dupes of subversives. This simplistic approach reinforces the convenient belief that advocates of social, military, or political reforms are as dangerous to the state as armed guerrillas.

Even more simplistic is the only human rights component of the school's sniper course: If, during their final exams, trainees fire on civilian targets, they fail the course. In fact, when Honduran and Colombian soldiers ran through "urban-combat exercises using blanks in their weapons, half the time, the village priest [played by a U.S. Army chaplain] is killed or roughed up."

HUMAN RIGHTS

Former SOA commandant, José Feliciano, who oversaw the training of hundreds of Salvadoran soldiers during his tenure, staunchly maintained that the human rights records of SOA client nations were beyond reproach... The current SOA commandant, Colonel José Alvarez, maintains the same line. "[SOA] probably does more in the area of teaching human rights than any other school in the world," he insists. The Colonel must have been on leave every time the 1989 murder in El Salvador of six Jesuit priests, their housekeeper, and her 16-year-old daughter, was mentioned. The Truth Commission implicated 27 soldiers and the Salvadoran courts convicted four in that massacre; 19 of the soldiers were SOA graduates...

SCHOOL FOR THUGS

Of the 27 Salvadorans fingered by the United Nations last year as responsible for the 1989 Jesuit murders, 19 were graduates of the Fort Benning School of the Americas. Ten of the 12 Salvadorean officers cited for the 1982 El Mozote massacre of 600 civilians were trained there.

A 1992 report by a coalition of human rights groups charged that of 246 Colombian human rights violators, 105 were School of Americas graduates.

In the "Hall of Fame" — a corridor in the school decorated with portraits of grads who, by the U.S. Army's dim lights, ascended to the heights — are generals from Bolivia, Guatemala, Honduras, Colombia and other Latin governments who killed or tortured their own people. Between 1,500 and 2,000 Latin American soldiers a year attend this school for brutality. It was founded by the U.S. Army in Panama in 1946 and moved to Fort Benning in 1984. In 48 years, some 58,000 Latins have been its students.

Army cosmeticians prettify this moral swamp as "a success story," one that promotes "military professionalism" and which has significantly contributed to the democratization of Latin America."

Colman McCarthy, **The Washington Post**, May 4, 1994.

Thus, the U.S. Army School of the Americas–by honing the military skills and rewarding the atrocities of this hemisphere's most brutal armed forces–undermines the human rights it purports to instill. At best, the low-intensity conflict it teaches maintains the status quo in nations with large, impoverished populations plagued by unfair labor practices, poor living conditions, and lack of education; at worst, it is a tool for achieving and legitimizing fascism.

As the U.N. Truth Commission Report on El Salvador clearly demonstrates, SOA training does not alter the patterns of traditionally abusive militaries–it only makes the alumni more mindful of hiding their atrocities. Shutting the doors on the U.S. Army School of the Americas would save millions of dollars–and perhaps thousands of lives.

24 THE POLITICS OF TERROR

TRAINING LEADERS
FOR THE FUTURE

Russell W. Ramsey

Russell W. Ramsey, Ph.D., is a distinguished resident professor at the U.S. Army School of the Americas.

Points to Consider:

1. What current myth does the author describe?

2. How is the military in Latin America portrayed?

3. Summarize the mission of the U.S. Army's School of the Americas.

4. Who are the opponents of the School of the Americas and what do they say?

5. Why should the School of the Americas stay open?

Russell W. Ramsey, "Assembly's Call to Close School of Americas Challenged," **The Presbyterian Layman,**, September/October 1994. Reprinted with permission.

More Panamanians learned to operate engineer equip-
ment at the School of the Americas than graduated
from all technical schools in that country.

A current myth maintains that Uncle Sam spends millions of tax dollars to train soldiers and police in Latin America for bad reasons, and that these 55,000 alumni then use this training to topple governments, murder spokesmen for the poor, and wreck the democratic process. The main instrument of this wickedness is purported to be the School of the Americas at Ft. Benning, Ga. Deceived into believing this fantasy, the 1994 General Assembly of the Presbyterian Church (USA) voted 373-132 to call for the closure of the School of the Americas...

THE MILITARY IN LATIN AMERICA

Latin America, compared to Asia, Europe, Africa, and the Middle East, has been less warlike and less militarized since 1500 than any other world region. I have measured this in number of wars, number of people killed in wars, percent of public funds spend for arms, percent of men in military uniform, and military penetration into the civilian culture...

Latin American soldiers are negatively perceived because of the *leyenda negra,* a cruel British prejudice dating from Elizabethan times, strengthened by Oliver Cromwell, and perpetuated by intellectuals in the present under the guise of neo-Marxist thought. Under this concept, all Latin American military people are either vicious, cowardly killers, or ridiculous figures like the fat sergeant on the television series *Zorro.* It is easier to say "I don't like Latin American military people" than "I'm prejudiced against Latin Americans." Most Latin American countries have public opinion polls showing support for their small, relatively benign military forces.

The Age of Gunboat Diplomacy (1890-1931) put the United States into northern Latin America as armed peacemaker and power broker, but not into continental South America. The Cold War (1947-1989) projected the United States into Latin America militarily in two ways. Until Cuba chose sides with the Soviet Union in 1960, the United States wrongly and foolishly backed armed dictators in Guatemala, Cuba, Nicaragua, the Dominican Republic, Venezuela, and briefly in Colombia, and to a lesser degree elsewhere. Once Fidel Castro developed an apparatus for projecting armed revolution, there really was an armed threat, a Cold War threat, in the region, and U.S. military assistance programs took on stronger moral validity.

From 1947-1989, about 2 percent of all U.S. military assistance worldwide, and 4 percent of foreign arms sales worldwide, went to Latin America. And throughout it all, the U.S. Army was the main agent of contact with Latin America soldiers, walking a delicate line between military interference in government and needed steps to oppose armed Marxist revolutionaries. Much polarization took place, not just in Latin America but among U.S. Christians. Some tried to justify Marxist revolution as part of Jesus' compact with the poor, and some tried to justify right-wing dictators as biblically necessary. Both were wrong, and the U.S. Army walked this tightrope with skill and sensitivity.

SCHOOL OF THE AMERICAS

The U.S. Army School of the Americas began in 1947 in Panama to help the Latin Americans with technical training. For example, during the 1960s more Panamanians learned to operate engineer equipment at the School of Americas than graduated from all technical schools in that country. Attorney General Robert Kennedy hailed the school as a necessary dimension of the Alliance for Progress...

Vicious misbehavior in uniform by the El Salvadoran Army, 1981-1989, was countered by a small on-site U.S. Army mission; by training at the School of the Americas (moved to Ft. Benning in 1984); and by unit package training. At war's end there, the rebel Marti National Liberation Front (FMLN) Marxist guerrillas were part of the political process; the Army was cut by over half (with several offenders in prison), and a National Police force was under development.

The U.S. Army School of the Americas has always given human rights awareness training. Since everything is taught in Spanish, among fellow Latin Americans, with a multinational faculty, the training is quite good. But this training is cognitive, not affective; and the United States does not command the soldiers and police who receive the training. Overall, the School of the Americas has greatly helped those countries having vicious military personnel; and most Latin American countries do not have abusers in uniform at all. Their militaries are the world's smallest by percent of population, and they serve well in 12 of 23 Blue Helmet peacekeeping operations, often at host-country request.

IDEOLOGICAL OPPOSITION

The little group of Maryknoll activists (a secular organization no longer recognized as a religious order by the Catholic Church) advocating closure of the School of the Americas is seeking vengeance for past abuses by the El Salvadoran military. These Maryknolls prey upon ignorance, myths, and the good intentions of U.S. Christians, while others serve faithfully as ordained priests. They support armed Marxist revolution by the FMLN. But the scene has changed. El Salvador is an emerging democracy, at peace, and we do not design our policies for just one country in Latin America but rather for the whole region.

The Western Hemisphere is the world's model of emerging democracy under free enterprise economies, with small, apolitical armed forces doing mostly humanitarian and public order jobs. These forces both need and benefit from the U.S. Army School of the Americas, more so now than during the Cold War. They have to fight the drug lords, and all nations have a right to maintain armed forces to express their sovereignty. Many are converting their armies to national police, on the model of the Costa Rican Civil Guards. The school's annual budget is less than that of a small junior college. In return, it averts wars that cost half a billion dollars a day.

CLOSING THE SCHOOL

If we were to close the School of the Americas for the few bad apples among its graduates, we would have to close several other institutions first. For example, Heidelberg University produced Joseph Goebbels, spiritual architect of the anti-Jewish Holocaust. Edinburgh University, that bastion of Presbyterianism, produced Lord Palmerston, architect of the Opium War against China. And Harvard graduated Admiral Yamamoto, who planned the Japanese attack on Pearl Harbor.

Heidelberg, Edinburgh, and Harvard each had several years to train their infamous graduates. By contrast, General Galtieri, who misgoverned Argentina badly and led them into the Malvinas/Falklands war, only had four weeks in a technical course at the School of the Americas, four decades before seizing power. Shall we shut down the brilliantly successful U.S. Job Corps because a few graduates became criminals? Should we label Colombian Army officers, known as world leaders in human rights circles, as moral offenders in need of sermons from U.S. Christians? They, after all, are fighting the horrible drug war created in their land by the cash from U.S. narcotics addicts.

The School of the Americas invites all Presbyterians to visit, to view the curriculum, to meet the students, and, most importantly, to witness the work done by the graduates in their own countries. I see them as professionals who try to follow God's mandates carefully; they honor us by coming here for a brief schooling experience. Other countries far less moral on military and police matters are offering them free courses. They come here precisely because we care about human rights as well as technical excellence. They sometimes ask me why U.S. Christians, who oppose prejudice, are so prejudiced against them as a class. (Currently, 10 majors and lieutenant colonels from the Command and General Staff College class are devoting their Saturdays to helping flood victims in Albany, Ga., 90 miles away, repair their flood-damaged homes.)

I doubt that Presbyterians, knowing all the facts, will want to send them away.

RECOGNIZING AUTHOR'S POINT OF VIEW

This activity may be used as an individualized study guide for students in libraries and resource centers or as a discussion catalyst in small group and classroom discussions.

The capacity to recognize an author's point of view is an essential reading skill. Many readers do not make clear distinctions between descriptive articles that relate factual information and articles that express a point of view. Think about the readings in Chapter Three. Are these readings essentially descriptive articles that relate factual information or articles that attempt to persuade through editorial commentary and analysis?

Guidelines

1. Read through the following source descriptions. Choose one of the source descriptions that best describes each reading in Chapter Three.

Source Descriptions

   a. Essentially an article that relates factual information

   b. Essentially an article that expresses editorial point of view

   c. Both of the above

   d. None of the above

2. After careful consideration, pick out one reading in Chapter Three that you agree with the most. Be prepared to explain

148

the reasons for your choice in a general class discussion.

3. Choose source descriptions above that best describe the other readings in this book.

4. Summarize the author's point of view in one sentence for each of the following readings in Chapter Three.

Reading 15 _____

_____

_____

Reading 16 _____

_____

_____

Reading 17 _____

_____

_____

Reading 18 _____

_____

_____

Reading 19 _____

_____

_____

Reading 20 _____

_____

_____

CHAPTER 4

HUMANITARIAN INTERVENTION

25 HUMANITARIAN INTERVENTION

PREVENTING GENOCIDE IN RWANDA

Holly Burkhalter

Holly Burkhalter wrote the following in her capacity as Director of Human Rights Watch. She made her statement before a House Foreign Affairs Subcommittee chaired by Tom Lantos of California.

Points to Consider:

1. Why is genocide the right name for what happened in Rwanda?

2. What political factors in Rwanda led to the genocide?

3. How did U.S. policy toward Rwanda fail?

4. Could steps have been taken by the U.S. and/or other nations that would have prevented the tragedy of genocide?

Excerpted from Congressional testimony by Holly Burkhalter before the House Foreign Affairs Subcommittee on International Security, International Organizations and Human Rights, February 1 and May 10, 1994.

The proper name for what is going on in Rwanda is "genocide."

American policy and international policy toward Rwanda is really about calling something by its real name and that is what human rights reporting should be; calling things by their proper name. And the proper name for what is going on in Rwanda is "genocide." That is not a word that Human Rights Watch uses lightly ever.

But when as much as a fifth of the country's population has been targeted for extermination; when soldiers and militia men go into an orphanage and take out a couple dozen Tutsi children and slaughter them before their Hutu playmates; when people's identity cards are checked at a checkpoint, the Hutus are permitted to go past, the Tutsis are slaughtered on the spot, then it is time to call this atrocity by its real name.

By calling the situation in Rwanda "genocide" that does not mean that it does not also have a political component to it. It is "genocide" in service of a higher political end, I should say, lower political end, that political end being control of the Rwandan Government, which is what this band of military thugs and their civilian supporters were attempting to do. They are using the scapegoating and targeting of a vulnerable minority people and a moderate political opposition, which includes many Hutus, to that end.

It occurs to me that if the U.S. Government had led the international community in calling this atrocity by its real name, we would have seen some serious action to put a stop to it. Because, indeed, we are not just morally obliged to put a stop to it, we are legally obliged to do so, as you well know, under the terms of the Genocide Convention, which we have ratified. But we have not called it by its name, and I think that is because the United States has no intention of complying with its legal obligations to suppress, prevent and punish this greatest of crimes.

The question of proper policy on Rwanda has focused, of course, on the role of UN forces there. My organization was aghast and heartbroken when the Clinton administration took the decision to draw down the UN forces, even while we acknowledged that they were not able to carry out their original cease-fire monitoring role.

"HANG ON A MINUTE—HERE COMES INDIFFERENCE...."

Cartoon by John Trever.

WITHDRAWING FORCES

We felt very strongly that they were playing an important role and continue to play that role. We felt it was a terrible signal at the height of the atrocities to draw the troops down to a skeleton number, a policy pushed forward by our own government at the Security Council. It was a signal to the mass murderers that there was not even a minimal presence to protect Rwandans.

The decision to draw down the forces was explained on practical grounds that there was fear for their security. Ten Belgian peacekeepers were mutilated and slaughtered as they attempted to protect the Hutu Prime Minister–they were murdered appallingly by the Rwandan Army on the first day of the outbreak of the crisis. That is not an idle matter when you lose 10 peacekkeepers.

However, speaking respectfully and regretfully about that, at the same time, it is important to keep this in perspective. In the 3 weeks thereafter, some 200,000 Rwandans lost their lives and not a single additional peacekeeper was killed; some were wounded.

PROTECTING INNOCENTS

However, given the absence of subsequent attacks on the peacekeepers, I think that their vulnerability needed to be weighted against the certainty of slaughter of those under their immediate protection. Now, of course, in the wake of massive atrocities, and I hope international embarrassment about it, there is endless dithering at the UN about enhancing the force gain. They should never have been drawn down in the first place.

I can get back to the protection issue, but I think it is important to note that no one in his right mind suggests that the UN forces should have imposed themselves between warring parties. It is essential to recognize that the mass number of those slaughters in Rwanda were not killed in the context of a conflict; they were not killed in the areas of fire from both sides; they were butchered by the tens of thousands in situations where there was no conflict.

Leaving aside the UN force issue, which is a difficult one, there were all kinds of things that did not cost a cent, did not put a single soldier in a danger, that could have been done if this matter had been of urgency to this administration and to other governments. We could have denounced by name those who are known to be responsible and made their names known in every foreign capital in the world.

I am happy to say that Anthony Lake, the National Security Advisor did name the names, at our request, of the military high command. He did not denounce them as being responsible for genocide, but he did call upon them to take every action in their power to end the massacres. It was a very welcome departure from normal protocol.

MORE NEEDED

However, much more was needed under the circumstances. His call should have been echoed by heads of state everywhere. The United States could have made an important contribution with other foreign donors to Rwanda, the Belgians, the French, and the World Bank, by making a public statement that no government which comes to power this way will ever receive a cent of foreign assistance. That was not done.

It is important and relevant because this is really about a power struggle, about a band of people that want to have their hands on

154

EXODUS

More than 1 million Hutus fled to Zaire and others to Tanzania in fear of retribution from Tutsi rebels who ousted a Hutu government that had orchestrated the slaughter of at least 500,000 Rwandans, most of them Tutsis, earlier this year.

"Rwandans Flee to Zaire," **Associated Press**, October 12, 1994.

the instruments of power, because that is the only way to make money in Rwanda. There was no high level attention to Rwanda until finally and belatedly the State Department dispatched John Shattuck to go not to Rwanda, but adjoining countries, and raise the human rights issue at a fairly high level. I think that was about a month overdue, though, very welcome when it did come. I think that the United States should have led the call that Amnesty International made for a special session of the UN Human Rights Commission.

Why is it that the highest level person that pays attention is an Assistant Secretary? Why have we not had Presidential proclamations? Why have we not had the United States insisting that the United Nations withdraw an utterly incompetent special envoy to Rwanda, who has been utterly irrelevant to helping solve this problem; why has this not been a matter of urgent attention even beyond the issue of the troops? There are many answers, but I think that we have to look at these mechanisms. We have to look beyond the reporting, beyond the rhetoric and beyond the speeches for ways that we can get our Government to do what needs to be done and to do it quickly, and in consultation with other governments. The Rwanda spectacle has been a disgrace and a disaster. The largest carnage in the shortest period of time, certainly in my experience in the human rights field, makes one reflect on Cambodia and Uganda and some of the other great disasters in human history. The fact that this has barely made a ripple in our policymaking is worthy of investigation.

26 HUMANITARIAN INTERVENTION

WE WERE RIGHT NOT TO FIGHT IN RWANDA

Samuel Francis

Samuel Francis wrote this statement as a syndicated article for PBJ Enterprises, Inc. It was reprinted from the Conservative Chronicle.

Points to Consider:

1. What is the UN Genocide Treaty?

2. How is this treaty defined?

3. Summarize the case against intervention in Rwanda.

4. Why is the UN Genocide Treaty unenforceable?

Samuel Francis, "White House Position on Genocide Isn't Clear," **Conservative Chronicle**, June 29, 1994. Reprinted by permission: **Tribune Media Services.**

The Clinton administration, we are relieved to note, seems unwilling to go to war in Rwanda.

Having brought the nation close to the brink of war with North Korea, planned a war with Haiti, toyed with war in the Balkans and actually botched a war in Somalia, the Clinton administration, we are relieved to note, seems unwilling to go to war in Rwanda. Since its reluctance suggests that there is after all some limit to the administration's recklessness in babbling about war, this is progress.

One bad reason for going to war in Rwanda is the UN Convention on the Prevention and Punishment of the Crime of Genocide, or "Genocide Treaty," a surpassingly foolish document forged by the United Nations and, after decades of controversy, ratified by the United States under President Reagan. The Genocide Treaty creates the legal offense of "genocide," defined as "acts committed with the intent to destroy, in whole or in part, a national, ethnic, racial or religious group" and obliges nations signing it to punish such acts.

The definition itself makes little sense, if only because by including destruction "in part" as an element of genocide, it means that the murder of any individual who is "part" of a "national, ethnic, racial or religious group" (whatever those are; they're not defined at all) could be construed as an act of genocide. But if the concept of genocide includes any murder, it becomes meaningless.

GENOCIDE TREATY

Critics of the treaty often pointed that out, but the Genocide Treaty had long been an ideological pet rock of liberals, and the liberal hysteria to pass it was so intense that the treaty's critics were accused of secretly sympathizing with genocide. That, you know, is what liberals like to call "reasoned argument." Nevertheless, critics knew not only that the treaty's pretentious language was meaningless, but also that the treaty itself was meaningless, too. The current quibble over Rwanda tells us why.

Some estimates put the slaughter of Rwanda's Tutsi people by its Hutu people at more than 500,000 so far, and that's pretty clearly genocide by any definition. Under the Genocide Treaty, we, the United States, and all the other signatory nations are obligated to punish the perpetrators. That means a military expe-

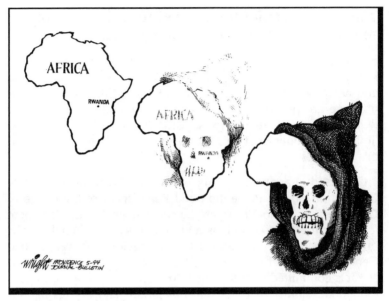

Cartoon by Richard Wright.

dition to Rwanda to nab the genocide committers, put them on trial and punish them. As with most politicized justice, there would be little practical question of guilt or innocence, let alone of fair trial procedures. Invigorated by progressivist bloodlust, we couldn't allow ourselves to be distracted by such things.

HUMAN RIGHTS

But, while "human rights activists" and all the rest of the legion of international busybodies are all for an immediate crusade in Rwanda to stop the genocide, cooler heads know very well it's not a good idea. We have absolutely no interests in Rwanda. Few Americans know where it is or care, a military expedition there would be difficult if not impossible and the whole business would set a bad precedent that might lead us into similar boondoggles. Why, the next thing you know we might be sending troops to Somalia.

What this means, then, is that the Genocide Treaty is unenforceable and therefore meaningless. It does nothing to stop or punish genocide. All it does or ever did was allow liberals to slap themselves on their backs for being "against genocide," let them preach and strut about how benevolent they are, and lob smears at the treaty's critics for being "pro-genocide." But the treaty itself is a fraud, and the weasel words of the Clinton Administration over Rwanda prove it beyond dispute.

ACTS OF GENOCIDE

The Administration claims that while "acts of genocide" have occurred in Rwanda, "genocide" has not occurred. Asked by the press "how many acts of genocide does it take to make genocide," the administration spokeswoman replied she wasn't in a position to answer. Now the Administration, and probably the United States itself, finds itself exposed to the ridicule of the world, because it has to resort to such transparent distortion of the meaning of genocide to avoid embroiling itself in a military adventure that is so clearly irrelevant and harmful to our interests and needs as a nation.

And that, of course, is a very compelling reason we should never have signed the Genocide Treaty at all: It obliges us to do what we can't and don't want to do and serves to trivialize and discredit our own laws and our own seriousness as a nation when we don't abide by its obligations. You don't have to be soft on genocide to believe the Genocide Treaty is a stupid and harmful idea, but you do need to be more serious about the rule of law and national interest than those who so passionately demanded we sign it.

27 HUMANITARIAN INTERVENTION

CHINA (MFN) AND HUMAN RIGHTS: THE POINT

Senator Bill Bradley

Bill Bradley is a Democratic Senator from the state of New York. The following is excerpted from a speech before the United States Senate on May 18, 1994.

Points to Consider:

1. Summarize the nature of America's China policy in the last 40 years.

2. Discuss the nature of the Deng Xiaoping economic reforms in China.

3. How have these reforms led to more freedom?

4. Why should Most Favored Nation status (MFN) not be linked to human rights progress in China?

5. What kind of trade restrictions does Senator Bradley say are justified to promote human rights in China?

6. How is an effective human rights policy toward China defined?

Excerpted from a Senate speech by Senator Bill Bradley on May 18, 1994.

Link specific sanctions to specific problems, not to human rights in general.

On June 3, President Clinton will determine the fate of China's Most Favored Nation trade status. Although the issue has been framed in terms of trade and human rights, in fact the choice is between two competing views of America's relationship with China. The President will be choosing whether to free China policy from the Cold War straight jacket embodied in the Most Favored Nation (MFN) human rights linkage. He should end the linkage and free American policy to pursue a more multi-faceted approach to U.S.-China relations. *(Editor's note: on June 3, 1994, President Clinton ended this linkage.)*

For over 40 years, America's China policy was subordinated to the Cold War struggle between liberal market democracy and communist totalitarianism. After failing to prevent the "fall" of China in 1949, the U.S. worked to isolate and exclude "Red China" from the international community. Then, after over 20 years of a China policy that tried to pretend that the world's most populous country did not exist, President Nixon played the "China Card" against the Soviet Union, starting a process which led to full diplomatic relations in 1979.

Just as the U.S. established full diplomatic relations with the People's Republic of China, Deng Xiaoping unleashed the first of the reforms that would open China to the world and transform it from a "command society" built around a centralized bureaucracy and communist economy, to a primarily market economy.

ECONOMIC GROWTH

Deng's reforms have turned China into an economic giant. Using purchasing power parities, the World Bank has determined that China is already the world's third largest economy. That may be stretching the point but, by any measure, it is clear that China is a major economic power.

Growing at over 10% per year, China has become an important engine for global economic growth. For example, China is America's fastest growing export market. American exports to the People's Republic rose by 18% last year to $8.8 billion, triple the figure of a decade ago, making China our 13th largest export market. Even that figure may be an understatement, when reports through Hong Kong are taken into account. U.S. companies have

'WHY DO I GET THE FEELING NOBODY TAKES ME SERIOUSLY?'

also committed billions in investment in China. America's strategy for export-led growth requires continued economic engagement with China.

COLD WAR

However, there is a residual Cold War-era trap which could slow this progress and put the U.S. at odds with the forces transforming China–the linkage of MFN and human rights. This linkage embodies two aspects of Cold War old-think, both of which should join the Cold War on the dust heap of history.

The time is past due to escape this trap and turn the page to a new policy framework that will do justice to the importance of the U.S.-China relationship. For America has a big stake in a healthy U.S.-China relationship. Without responsible Chinese behavior, no stable Asian security equilibrium is possible. Without responsible Chinese behavior, America cannot manage its regional and global security agenda. Trade, the future of Hong Kong and Taiwan, North Korean proliferation, environmental degradation–all require Chinese cooperation. Because China is a veto-wielding permanent member of the United Nations Security

Council, Chinese cooperation is vital for the American global agenda from Bosnia to Iraq.

I strongly agree with those who contend that we have an important national interest in improving the living conditions of China's 1.2 billion people. Support for the dignity of the individual is part of who we are as a nation. However, the MFN-human rights linkage has provided too narrow a path to try to influence Beijing's human rights practices. We need a more multi-faceted approach that works with the forces shaping China, not against them.

HUMAN RIGHTS

An effective human rights policy must be based on measures to increase China's exposure to the outside world. Expanding *Voice of America* and *Radio Free Asia* broadcasts would swell the flow of unbiased information into China, including much-needed information about Tibet. Increasing educational and cultural exchanges would expose more Chinese, especially in the younger generation, to our example as a multi-ethnic, multi-cultural, stable, and prosperous democracy. The more U.S. delegations go to China with open access to factories, farms, and businesses, the deeper will be the human rights message.

Human rights policy must also seek to expand trade. Trade is the motive force behind China's opening to the world. That is why I support China's membership in the World Trade Organization. China's obligations as a WTO member would require Beijing to replace policy with law in the economic sphere, even as it encouraged China's continued economic dynamism. Growth alone will not democratize China. But it does create the fluid political and social environment, the exposure to the outside world, and the emergence of a class of economically prosperous Chinese, which are the prerequisites for democratization and improved human rights practices.

The alternative, disrupting trade in support of human rights goals, would work against the forces that are liberalizing China. It would run counter to the efforts of the Chinese people themselves to better their lot. It would create an "American recession" in south China that could turn individual Chinese against us.

Another element of human rights policy is genuine dialogue. All too often, the U.S.-China human rights "dialogue" consists of American officials presenting Chinese counterparts with a list of demands. China, supported by other Asians, has responded that "Western" human rights standards are not applicable in Asia. The result has been an empty exchange of monologues.

The alternative is genuine exchange with the Chinese and other Asians on human rights. While we will not agree with Asian assertions about the relativity of human rights, we can hear them out with the aim of finding common ground on which to build. We can begin by framing some essential human rights principles, such as rule of law, in positive terms. Rule of law is not only in the interests of Chinese, it is in the interest of whoever is governing China. How can China be governed or China's economy be managed without rule of law?

As we wait for the last members of the Long March generation to pass from the scene, we must continue our efforts to protect individual Chinese dissidents, such as Wei Jingsheng, by raising their cases at every opportunity and working to improve conditions in detention.

ESTABLISHING A DIALOGUE

Tough talk on individual cases does not contradict my call for genuine dialogue. Rather, once we are talking effectively with the Chinese, appeals on behalf of individual dissidents will have greater impact as part of this genuine dialogue. There are many ways to institutionalize such a dialogue, such as by creating a binational human rights commission or exchanging parliamentary delegations to investigate human rights practices, as the Chinese and Australians now do.

China's craving for international legitimacy provides additional influence. As part of our human rights framework, we must make it clear to Beijing that we will work to deny China the symbols of full international legitimacy as long as China fails to uphold basic human rights standards. That is why I worked to deny China the 2000 Olympics and will, if necessary, work to deny China the 2004 Olympics. China should not host UN agency meetings as long as it abuses its people. For example, China is slated to host the Fourth World Conference on Women next year in Beijing. This is the kind of meeting we must deny Beijing until its human rights practices improve.

We must also ask business to help by supporting international voluntary ethical investor principles, preferably as part of an investment code. This would harness international business in pursuit of practices that encourage China's liberalization, without putting our firms at a competitive disadvantage. This code would not be, as business may fear, a unilateral requirement for business to bear the brunt of Washington's human rights agenda. Nor would it imply that business is a key part of the solution.

MULTILATERAL ACTION

Notice how many of the steps I have outlined call for action in a multilateral context. This is no coincidence. For our credibility and impact, we must eliminate the appearance that human rights is only a bizarre American preoccupation and actively seek out ways to exert concerted Asian and international pressure on Beijing.

Proposals for partial or targeted revocation of MFN have no place in this framework. Conceptually, such an approach is wrong because it would maintain the trade-human rights link. It would hurt U.S. business and consumers, run counter to the forces transforming China, and still leave the Administration looking weak. Tactically, there is no reason to believe China would cave in to partial revocation if the threat of full revocation was ineffective.

That does not mean there is no place for sanctioning specific Chinese products. Products made with prison or child labor should be sanctioned. If the Administration wants to exclude the Chinese-made AK-47's that are coming into this country as so-called "sporting rifles," it should by all means do so. But link specific sanctions to specific problems, not to human rights in general. A decision to revoke or continue to condition China's MFN status would be a blunder of historic proportions. In post-Cold War Asia, we would be isolating ourselves from the world's most dynamic region. We would be standing alone against the forces transforming China, Asia, and the world. The Cold War is over. Let us put it behind us, delink MFN from human rights, and begin to realize the potential of the U.S.-China relationship.

CHINA (MFN) AND HUMAN RIGHTS: THE COUNTERPOINT

Robin Munro

Robin Munro is the primary China researcher for Asia Watch based in Hong Kong. Asia Watch is a division of Human Rights Watch, a non-governmental human rights monitoring organization.

Points to Consider:

1. How are human rights violations in China described?

2. What is the relationship between economic reform and human rights in China?

3. Summarize the nature of U.S. policy toward human rights in China.

4. Describe the proper relationship between U.S. trade policy and human rights in China.

5. Under what circumstances should Most Favored Nation (MFN) status be granted to China?

Excerpted from Congressional testimony by Robin Munro before the House Foreign Affairs Subcommittee on Asia and Pacific Affairs of the House Foreign Affairs Committee, May 20, 1993.

*There is a mistaken tendency on the part of some poli-
cy makers to equate moves towards economic reform
with political liberalization in China.*

We are particularly grateful to you for providing this occasion to
spotlight human rights violations in China and Tibet, because the
situation remains among the worst in the world. Gross abuses
continue, thousands of political prisoners are held in squalor and
misery, and many more are required to work in forced labor
camps. Freedom of assembly, expression, and religion are brutal-
ly suppressed, independent human rights organizations continue
to be crushed, and access by international human rights and
humanitarian groups to labor camps, prisons, and other places of
detention is denied.

There is a mistaken tendency on the part of some policy makers
to equate moves towards economic reform and modernization
with political liberalization in China. Recent events should
remove any such delusions. Notwithstanding Deng Xiaoping's
highly publicized tour of southern China in late January 1992 and
the subsequent wave of economic reforms, political repression
continued unabated.

The year 1992 witnessed the crushing of a number of pro-
democracy groups which emerged from the ashes of Tiananmen
Square. Asia Watch learned of the secret arrest of some 40
human rights activists associated with progressive groups that
sprang up in 1992.

U.S. POLICY

Asia Watch is disappointed that the United States Government
has been largely silent on the subject of human rights in China.
Asia Watch had hoped that the new Administration would put
maximum pressure on Beijing to make human rights concessions.
In our view, the Chinese might have felt it necessary to make
major human rights concessions before Most Favored Nation
(MFN) renewal if the President had spoken publicly about human
rights concerns early in his term and indicated precisely what
steps on human rights the Chinese must take if MFN was to be
renewed.

Unfortunately, there has been no major speech on China and
no public identification of what steps China must take if MFN was
to be renewed. Nor has the executive branch raised tariffs selec-

tively on products under the authority of Section 301 of the Trade Act. And the Clinton Administration has not been any more vigorous on prohibiting the importation of products made by forced labor than was the Bush Administration. At any time , the Clinton Administration could have signalled its seriousness to the Chinese by invoking tariff increases or prohibiting shipments of forced labor-made products which would have indicated to Beijing that the United States has a new president, and it will not be business as usual.

MFN AND HUMAN RIGHTS

In calling upon the Clinton Administration to enact some kind of targeted trade sanctions, we are simply asking for the same approach on behalf of human rights that the U.S. has used quite effectively on commercial matters of concern. As you know, the United States threatened tariff increases on a range of Chinese Government-made products in late 1991 because of disputes over patent and copyright violations, and the Chinese quickly took action to correct the problem. The U.S. again threatened some $3.7 billion in trade sanctions against the Chinese in 1992 to force concessions on economic concerns, and again the Chinese responded favorably, signing a far-reaching agreement on market access and averting the imposition of sanctions. We have long recommended that the U.S. government take comparable action–threatening targeted trade sanctions short of eliminating MFN–to secure human rights concessions. We had hoped that it would be a tactic used by the Clinton Administration an indication that the U.S. is at least as serious about human rights as we are about patent and copyright violations.

While it appears unlikely that the Clinton Administration will take the step of imposing targeted tariff increases soon, we hope that it is something they will keep in mind if human rights deteriorate, as they did in 1992 with the arrests of dozens of pro-democracy demonstrators and organizers.

The important question for Congress is, what will be the conditions placed upon MFN renewal, and what mechanism will the executive branch use to monitor compliance with them? We believe that it is vital that when MFN renewal is announced, that the Clinton Administration make it plain that it will be evaluating human rights throughout the year, and that at any time of the year, targeted tariff increases are a possibility unless progress is made

Cartoon by Dick Locher. Reprinted with permission: **Tribune Media Services.**

on human rights conditions. China should not be given a free MFN ride for another calendar year. The Clinton Administration can enhance the chance of important human rights concessions, including prisoner releases, if it evaluates human rights periodically, and regularly reminds Beijing of the human rights conditions that it has placed on the MFN relationship.

RENEWING MFN

Asia Watch believes that the most important conditions to stress when MFN is renewed are the following:

1. Release of political prisoners and a full accounting including details on their legal status, places of detention, charges pending against them, restrictions following release;

2. Confidential and regular access to Chinese jails, prisons, and labor camps by international humanitarian organizations in order to help end torture and ill-treatment;

3. Opening up Tibet to access by foreign journalists and human rights monitors;

4. Easing legal restrictions on free religious belief outside the

control of official churches and ending the persecution of religious believers;

5. Full compliance with China's commitments to cease the export of prison-made goods to the U.S. and to allow unrestricted access to all prison facilities suspected of producing goods for export.

This last condition is an avenue for pressuring China that is particularly important. The U.S. and China reached a Memorandum of Understanding on August 7, 1992. Unfortunately, the MOU appears to have had almost no impact at all on the ability of the U.S. to monitor the production of made-for-export products in prison factories and farms. If the current MOU is inadequate to provide access to all places where prisoners are suspected of making products for export, then it should be re-negotiated. Again, banning the importation of categories of goods known to be produced in prison factories would be the most immediate way to signal U.S. seriousness on this important issue.

PRISON LABOR

Since Asia Watch first published confidential Chinese government documents in April 1991 describing the extent of prison labor exports to the U.S. and other foreign markets, we have supplied information to the Customs Service and to the State Department. We met most recently with Customs here in Washington, and I have regular contact with their offices in Hong Kong. When the MOU was first signed, we noted it was a positive step but expressed concern that the agreement was incredibly vague about the conditions for inspection; without such inspections, monitoring compliance is impossible.

Without that pressure, China has dragged its feet on complying with at least 18 requests for investigations and visits recently submitted by the U.S. Only a few inspections have been allowed, such as a visit to the Gold Horse Diesel Engine Factory last fall; but even in that case, access to the factory–part of Yunnan No. 1 Prison–was strictly limited.

The information released by Harry Wu underlines the urgent need to challenge China's reluctance to open up its prison farms and factories to outside inspection. Beijing claims it is against Chinese government policy to export prison products to the U.S. In that case, what are they hiding?

171

TIBET

All but 13 of Tibet's 6,254 temples have been reduced to rubble by the Chinese. More than 1 million Tibetans have been killed. Monks are still being tortured, and nuns raped. Ganden Monastery, which bustled two generations ago with the chanting of lamas, the cut and thrust of debate, the jostle of a thriving city on a hill, is little more now than broken walls. The Drepung, once the largest monastery in the world, carries no voice but the wind's.

The systematic desecration of Tibet has been continuing for 40 years. Now, though, an entirely new culture is being set up in its place. In order to adulterate the race, Beijing has flooded the area with Han Chinese, so that Tibetans are outnumbered in their capital 3-1. In the shadow of the 13-story Potala Palace, the rulers have erected a Holiday Inn. The land once known as Shambhala is home to more than 300,000 soldiers; Shangri-La is now a nuclear-testing site.

Pico Iyer, **Los Angeles Times**, 1990.

We received a letter smuggled out of Lingyuan Prison in northwest China, part of a huge prison complex involved in production for export. The letter, written by Liu Gang, a 32-year old student who was No. 3 on the "Most Wanted" list, is a dramatic cry for help to the international community. Liu is serving a six-year prison sentence. He has been repeatedly beaten and tortured with electric batons. According to his family, he is suffering from stomach and heart problems, and his hair, now one-third white, is beginning to fall out. He also is suffering from a prolapsed anus from being forced to sit on a narrow punishment bench. He has received no medical treatment.

Could this be what the Chinese are so anxious to keep hidden from the outside world?

WORLD BANK LOANS

Another important area for the Clinton Administration to pursue as a means of pressuring China on human rights is World Bank loans. The United States does not appear to be using its "voice and vote" to direct World Bank resources away from China, as human rights law requires. Thus even with the U.S. abstaining on loans to China, World Bank lending is now even higher than pre-Tiananmen levels. The Clinton Administration should be actively pursuing ways of directing World Bank resources away from China, rather than merely abstaining on loans which sail through without our support, which was the Bush Administration's approach. The Clinton Administration has a tremendous opportunity to bring pressure on China which may secure the release of hundreds of men and women attempting to create civil society and democratic organizations within China.

29   HUMANITARIAN INTERVENTION

INTERVENTION IN THE BALKANS IS JUSTIFIED

Paul C. Warnke

Paul C. Warnke is a former Assistant Secretary of Defense for International Affairs.

Points to Consider:

1. Define the post-war risks to allied security.

2. How has the North Atlantic Treaty Organization (NATO) responded to these risks?

3. What is the cause of the tragedy in Bosnia?

4. How should NATO respond to Serbian aggression in Bosnia?

5. Why does the author call for military intervention in Bosnia by NATO forces?

Excerpted from Congressional testimony by Paul C. Warnke before the Commission on Security and Cooperation in Europe, July 21, 1993.

The moral imperative is clear. The security threat is real. The time for action is now.

MEMBERS OF THE COMMISSION:

You have asked for my views regarding American interests in the post-Cold War Europe and how these interests might be affected if the present Balkan conflict were to spread. You have also asked me to comment on the role the NATO alliance should play in ending the bloodshed in the former Yugoslavia, particularly in Bosnia.

NATO

Back in November, 1991, at a meeting in Rome, the NATO foreign ministers gave what I believe to be the proper analysis of these questions. They declared that, with the end of the Soviet threat, the real risks to allied security would arise from "the serious economic, social and political difficulties, including ethnic rivalries and territorial disputes, which are faced by many countries in Central and Eastern Europe." However, when confronted with the actuality of this anticipated post-Cold War threat, NATO has failed to respond with anything other than rhetoric.

Ironically, the NATO defense ministers, meeting in Brussels on May 26, 1993, called for an end to reductions in the military budgets of alliance members, noting that: "A stabilization of defense expenditures, as well as a more effective use of our national and collective resources, are necessary to enable the alliance to respond in a timely and effective way to the challenges of the future." But if NATO refuses to put its muscle where its mouth is, it's hard to see what we are spending our money for and why the alliance should survive. We are now confronted with just the sort of security threat for which NATO action is the best, if not the only, solution.

SERBIAN AGGRESSION

The Serbian aggression in Bosnia-Herzegovina and, to a lesser extent, Croatian complicity in it, has left NATO inert. The proposals that have been advocated, such as safe havens for the Muslim population, or the partition of Bosnia into ethnic enclaves, are no solution at all and could readily lead to further ethnic purges in an area of Europe characterized by states with a dazzling ethnic mix. Kosovo is an Albanian-populated enclave in Serbia. Macedonia is

175

Cartoon by Steve Sack. Reprinted with permission from **Star Tribune** , Minneapolis.

inhabited by Albanians, Bulgarians, Serbs and other ethnic minorities. Hungarians are dispersed all over what were the Austro-Hungarian and Ottoman empires.

Outside of the former Yugoslavia, in various of the former Soviet republics, people of differing cultural and genetic roots will either learn to live together or will massacre one another for reasons that having nothing to do with any pragmatic conflicts of interests. The very concept of the ethnic state is inconsistent with any sensible or sustainable world order.

In a recent speech here in Washington, Richard von Weizsacker, President of the Federal Republic of Germany, contrasted what is happening today in former Yugoslavia with the proper concept of a nation in today's world: "Cultural competition in a free society and across open frontiers works as a stimulating and unifying element. As we are sadly observing, it can, when used as an instrument for pretended superiority, exclusiveness and power turn into a cause for separation, hatred and even extermination. Culture guarded, defined and enshrined by national frontiers is a contradiction in terms to the culture we know and cherish: open, alive and international."

176

BOSNIA

Nor is it true that the incalculable human tragedy in Bosnia is the inevitable consequence of ancient hatreds. For generations, Serbs, Croats and Muslims have been able to live together in peace. What we are seeing today is the product of divisive and deceitful propaganda by rapacious leaders bent on enlarging their own spheres of domination regardless of the cost in human lives and misery.

NATO, led as necessary by strong U.S. prodding, must make it clear that murderous thuggery will not be tolerated and will instead be punished. Unless it does so, the alliance is a costly anachronism. It is, in my view, absurd to contend, as some of its members do, that NATO can do nothing because it was not intended to engage in military action "out of area." What used to be Yugoslavia has NATO countries to the east and to the south as well as to the west. If ethnic homogeneity is to be accepted as a prime criterion for statehood, then Europe can never be at peace and western European economic integration will not be sufficient to bring about prosperity and progress. For the western nations, including the United States, the resulting chaos will prevent the development of lucrative markets for our products and our technology.

I can take no comfort in the suggestions that Bosnia is a distant land or that this is a pot-and-kettle war where everyone is at fault. We have seen in the past—as when Nazi Germany invaded Czechoslovakia—that such assertions only succeeded in postponing action to stop aggression until the task of doing so had become exponentially more difficult.

MILITARY INTERVENTION

It is, regrettably, quite late in the game. With the advantage of hindsight, the international recognition of states seceding from Yugoslavia was premature and should have been preceded by negotiations designed to protect minority rights. Even then, a strong warning by the United States and its western allies against Serbian aggression might have frightened off that country's bully boys at an early stage. I can sympathize with the reluctance to initiate military action that may result in a long-term and even escalating engagement. But if aggression is allowed to go unchecked and unpunished in Europe, then NATO members, including the United States, will find themselves at some point

> # APPEASERS
>
> *At every past hint of firm international action, especially by the United States, the Serbs have pulled back. But there is practically nothing for them to fear now. In Europe and the United States, the appeasers have won.*
>
> Anthony Lewis, **New York Times**, December, 1993.

down the line involved in a wider war that might have been stifled with early action.

I believe we should call on NATO's military leaders to prepare, and pronounce a program for military intervention including, if necessary, the virtual occupation of Bosnia. Isolated or token military action is unlikely to help and could further endanger the United Nations peacekeeping forces. The more substantial the NATO military forces are, the less military opposition they will encounter and the greater the chance that political opposition within Serbia and Croatia may lead to more responsible governments. The program should be designed to break the siege of Sarajevo and other Bosnian cities and, if NATO forces meet with Serbian or Croatian resistance, to attack military targets of the aggressors within their own national borders.

The moral imperative is clear. The security threat is real. The time for action is now.

30 HUMANITARIAN INTERVENTION

IT'S TIME TO DISENGAGE FROM THE BALKANS

Doug Bandow

Doug Bandow is a syndicated columnist. He wrote the following article for the Copley News Service.

Points to Consider:

1. Why should the U.S. not intervene militarily in the Balkans?

2. Why should the arms embargo against the Bosnian Muslims be lifted?

3. Why should the arms embargo against Serbia be lifted?

4. What influence does the Serbian government have on the Bosnian Serbs?

Doug Bandow, "It Is Time to Disengage from the Balkans," **Conservative Chronicle**, August 8, 1994. Reprinted with permission of **Copley News Service**.

It should be painfully evident by now that the West cannot solve the bitter and brutal three-sided civil war that has been raging in the Balkans.

NATO has struck again in Bosnia, and at least this time blew up something more substantial than a couple of tents. But such pin-pricks will have no impact on the outcome of the Bosnian civil war. As one Clinton official admitted: "This is a momentary flare-up, not a turning point." Such flare-ups do, however, risk sucking the United States into deeper involvement in the Bosnian imbroglio. What do we do, for instance, if an American plane is shot down? We could easily find ourselves being pulled deeper into the conflict with no easy way out.

DISENGAGEMENT

It is time to disengage from the Balkans. First, the United States should lift the arms embargo on the Muslin-dominated Bosnian government. Let the Bosnian Muslims defend themselves. Like most civil wars, this one is tragic, but remains best left to the combatants to settle themselves, without outside interference.

Second, Washington should take the lead in dropping the economic embargo on Serbia. U.N. sanctions, imposed to punish Belgrade for having backed local Serb forces in both Croatia and Bosnia, have wrecked Serbia's economy. National income is estimated to have fallen at least 50 percent in the first two years. When I visited Serbia, Spasoje Spasojevic, secretary general of the Yugoslav National Committee of the International Chamber of Commerce, explained that eight of 10 firms had to shut down or drastically diminish operations.

WEALTH AND POVERTY

However, those with connections, influence and wealth–including leading government officials–remain relatively undisturbed. Mercedeses mix with Yugos on the street, and luxury goods are displayed in store windows. But the mass of people are not so lucky. The situation for some people is near catastrophe, since they lack the funds even to buy bread. Rev. Lazar Stojsic, a Pentecostalist minister, said that many members of his Belgrade congregation "can't afford clothes and shoes." It also is "very bad for the sick," he adds, who "can't afford to buy medicine if they can find it."

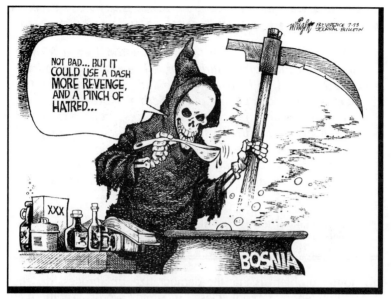

Cartoon by Richard Wright.

Neither of these men are fans of Serbian President Slobodan Milosevic. But sanctions have done nothing to loosen his hold on power. The United Nations may have hoped that the sanctions would cause people to rise up against Milosevic, but, explains Predrag Simic, head of the Institute of International Politics and Economics, "we Serbs like to be paranoid, believing that there is a conspiracy against us. The sanctions strengthen this feeling of paranoia." Not surprisingly, then, many Yugoslavs have rallied around their leaders. The Bush administration's attacks on Milosevic made people vote twice for the government.

SANCTIONS

At the same time the sanctions have undercut intellectuals around whom opposition to Milosevic could be expected to center. Because of sanctions, for instance, Simic's institute has had to abandon a European-oriented training program and drastically curtail its operations. Simic is no longer able to acquire American publications. International book and film festivals have been canceled, limiting religious as well as political exchange. The independent media has had to turn to the government to acquire newsprint.

DECLARE VICTORY AND LEAVE

Any proposed solution to the situation in the former Yugoslavia which will require Serbs to live in a state dominated by Muslims and Croats is doomed to failure. Even the Nazis failed to completely pacify Serbia. How then do we, with air strikes and "peace keeping" forces, propose to do so? The Balkans are not the Persian Gulf. The inevitable long and drawn-out parade of dead Americans that would follow from a policy of ever-increasing escalation will only exhaust the American people and cause us once again to "declare victory and leave."

Congressional Testimony by Bishop Anthony of the Greek Orthodox Archdiocese of North and South America, April 20, 1994.

Another problem is that the democratization "process depends on a strong enough middle class," in Simic's words. Yet these are the people most ravaged by a runaway inflation reminiscent of that in Weimar Germany during the early 1920s. Complains Simic, "We are losing all of the gains" of economic liberalization in our formerly communist nation.

More generally, the sanctions undercut democracy by reinforcing the government's economic hegemony: warns Vlajko Stojiljkovic, president of the Serbian Chamber of Commerce, sanctions are "counterproductive in developing both a market economy and pluralistic society." By destroying private firms, retarding privatization and severing international economic links, sanctions have fortified state influence over economic life.

THE SERBS

Moreover, as is evident from its break with Bosnian Serbs, there is little that the Milosevic government can do to stop the fighting around Sarajevo. Milosevic once had real influence over Serbs in the breakaway republic, but no longer. "Milosevic is more influenced by than an influence" on Bosnia, argues Simic. Of course, Serb behavior has often been atrocious. But no one's hands are clean. The Western allies have, for instance, quietly accepted Croatian brutality and ignored at least some Muslim responsibility in helping to create at least 265,000 largely Serbian refugees from that former Yugoslavian province.

It should be painfully evident by now that the West cannot solve the bitter and brutal three-sided civil war that has been raging in the Balkans. It's time to get out. And that includes lifting sanctions on Serbia. Today they achieve nothing, other than retarding movement toward both free markets and political democracy in Yugoslavia. And that is in no one's interest.

INTERPRETING EDITORIAL CARTOONS

This activity may be used as an individualized study guide for students in libraries and resource centers or as a discussion catalyst in small group and classroom discussions.

Although cartoons are usually humorous, the main intent of most political cartoonists is not to entertain. Cartoons express serious social comment about important issues. Using graphic and visual arts, the cartoonist expresses opinions and attitudes. By employing an entertaining and often light-hearted visual format, cartoonists may have as much or more impact on national and world issues as editorial and syndicated columnists.

Points to Consider

1. Examine the cartoon on page 181.

2. How would you describe the message of the cartoon? Try to describe the message in one to three sentences.

3. Do you agree with the message expressed in the cartoon? Why or why not?

4. Does the cartoon support the author's point of view in any of the readings in this publication? If the answer is yes, be specific about which reading or readings and why.

5. Are any of the readings in Chapter Four in basic agreement with the cartoon?

BIBLIOGRAPHY

Books on Torture and Human Rights

Amnesty International Report 1994. Amnesty International, New York: 1994.

Andersen, Martin E. **Dossier Secreto: Argentina's Desaparecidos and the Myth of the "Dirty War."** Westview: March 1993.

Bouvard, Marguerite G. **Revolutionizing Motherhood: The Mothers of the Plaza De Mayo.** Scholarly Res. Inc.: March 1994.

Emerson, Gloria. **Gaza: Year in the Intifada: A Personal Account.** Grover Atlantic: April 1992.

Harvest of Violence: The Maya Indians and the Guatemalan Crisis. Carmack, Robert, ed. University of Oklahoma Press: June 1988.

Human Rights Watch World Report 1994. Human Rights Watch, New York: 1994.

Millett, Kate. **The Politics of Cruelty: An Essay on the Literature of Political Imprisonment.** W. W. Norton and Company, New York: 1994.

A Modern Form of Slavery: Trafficking of Burmese Women and Girls into Brothels in Thailand. Asia Watch and the Women's Rights Project, ed. Human Rights Watch, New York: 1993.

Perera, Victor. **Unfinished Conquest: The Guatemalan Tragedy.** University of California Press: August 1993.

Simon, Jean-Marie. **Guatemala.** Norton: January 1988.

State of the Peoples: A Global Human Rights Report on Societies in Danger. Staff of Cultural Survival, ed. Beacon Press, Boston: 1993.

Stephens, Beth and Michael Ratner. **Suing for Torture and Other Human Rights Abuses in Federal Courts**. Transnational Publications: 1994.

Torture, Human Rights and Medical Ethics: The Case of Israel. Gordon, Neve and Ruchama Marton, ed. Humanities: April 1995.

Torture in Brazil: A Report. Catholic Church Staff. Random: October 1986.

War Crimes in Bosnia-Hercegovina. Staff-Helsinki Watch Report, ed. Human Rights Watch, New York: 1992.

Weschler, Lawrence. **A Miracle, a Universe: Settling Accounts with Torturers**. Pantheon: March 1990.

Wu, Hongda H. **Laogai–The Chinese Gulag**. Westview: March 1992.

Magazine Articles on Torture

Blundy, Anna. "Blow for Justice?" (corporal punishment for criminal offenses), **Guardian** (April 19, 1994): p2.

Davison, Phil. "Why Death Would Be a Victory for Ramon" (case of paralysed Spaniard seeking to be allowed to die), **Independent** (August 3, 1994): p11.

"Doctors Rebuff Police Torture Policy," **Facts on File** v53 (November 11, 1993): p855.

Drinan, Robert F. "A Mobilization of Shame" (Amnesty International's 1994 report), **Commonweal** v121 (October 7, 1994): p6.

Gordon, Myles. "Hot Spots" (countries where human rights are violated), **Scholastic Update** v126 (December 3, 1993): p4.

Gordon, Myles. "Shine a Light" (brutal torture of Kashmiri college student), **Scholastic Update** v126 (December 3, 1993): p17.

"Human Rights and the Chiapas Rebellion," **Current History** v93 (March 1994): p121.

"Lawyers Protest Alleged Torture Death" (Cairo, Egypt), **Facts on File** v54 (June 30, 1994): p466.

McShea, Daniel W. "On the Rights of an Ape," **Discover** v15 (February 1994): p34.

Nowak, Manfred. "States of Bondage," **UNESCO Courier** (March 1994): p28.

Pilger, John. "Deathly Silence of the Diplomats" (Britain condoning brutality of Indonesian regime), **Guardian** (October 12, 1994): p2.

Pilger, John. "Inside the Ministry of Propaganda" (how the UK Foreign Office avoids telling the truth about British support for the Khmer Rouge and British compliance in providing arms to the Indonesian occupiers of East Timor), **New Statesman & Society** v7 (April 29, 1994): p16.

Rugman, Jonathan. "Ankara Accused of Torture and Murder" (alleged abuses of human rights in Turkey), **Guardian** (June 22, 1994): p13.

Sweeney, John. "Torture Moves into the Shadows," **Observer** (December 12, 1993): p17.

"The Rights Row: China and America," **Economist** v330 (February 5, 1994): p32.

"The Seamy Underside of an Asian 'Miracle'" (Indonesia), **World Press Review** v41 (June 1994): p17.

Urquidi, Mariclaire Acosta, "Under the Volcano: Human Rights, Official Torture, and the Future of Mexican Democracy," **Humanist** v54 (November-December 1994): p26.

"Walk in Fear" (human rights in Iran), **Economist** v332 (July 23, 1994): p332.

Magazine Articles on Human Rights

Alibhai-Brown, Yasmin. "For Africa, the Only Answer Lies Within," **Independent** (October 26, 1994): p14.

"Appointment in Jakarta" (human rights in Indonesia), **America** v171 (November 19, 1994): p3.

"Being Too Diplomatic" (President Clinton fails to press human rights issues), **Nation** v259 (November 14, 1994): p561.

Bennoune, Karima. "Algerian Women Confront Fundamentalism," **Monthly Review** v46 (September 1994): p26.

"Breaking Free: An Anthology of Human Rights Poetry," **Publishers Weekly** v241 (October 31, 1994): p63.

Buchsbaum, Herbert. "Operation: Restore Democracy" (U.S. military intervention in Haiti), **Scholastic Update** v127 (November 4, 1994): p6.

Buckley, William F., Jr. "Castro and Pridefall," **National Review** v46 (September 26, 1994): p78.

"China: Medical-ethics Violations Charged" (charges that organs were transplanted from prisoners), **Facts on File** v54 (September 29, 1994): p714.

"Civil and Political Rights in the United States" (statement by John Shattuck), **U.S. Department of State Dispatch** v5 (September 19, 1994): p628.

Cleary, Edward L. "Struggling for Human Rights in Latin America," **America** v171 (November 5, 1994): p20.

Decter, Midge. "The State Department vs. America" (human rights report), **Commentary** v98 (November 1994): p65.

Drinan, Robert F. "Can Nations Make Amends for Crimes of the Past?" **National Catholic Reporter** v30 (September 30, 1994): p16.

Drinan, Robert F. "Why is the United States the World's Merchant of Death?" **America** v171 (September 24, 1994): p4.

Ehrlich, Paul. "Eric Lomax's Long Journey," **Reader's Digest** v145 (October 1994): p99.

Epstein, Jason. "Rethinking 'Schindler's List'," **Utne Reader** (July-August 1994): p136.

Kelley, Kevin J. "Are Western Ideas of Human Rights Alien to Asia?" **Utne Reader** (July-August 1994): p17.

Knippers, Diane. "Abusing Human Rights," **Christianity Today** v38 (October 3, 1994): p23.

Lindorff, Dave. "Ron Brown's 'lovefest' in Beijing," **Business Week** (September 12, 1994): p54.

McCrum, Robert. "New Light on East Timor," **Utne Reader** (November-December 1994): p46.

McGreal, Chris. "Hutu Homes Seized by Vengeful Tutsis," **Guardian** (November 22, 1994): p15.

"Myanmar: Dissident Meets Military Leaders," **Facts on File** v54 (September 29, 1994): p717.

Neier, Aryeh. "Watching Rights" (linkage between trade and human rights in China), **Nation** v259 (September 26, 1994): p299.

Nelan, Bruce W. "Business First, Freedom Second" (human rights and trade), **Time** v144 (November 21, 1994): p78.

O'Shaughnessy, Hugh. "Muslims Spit Hosts in Timor as Tension Grows" (East Timor), **National Catholic Reporter** v30 (September 9, 1994): p10.

"Rights vs. Responsibilities" (speech delivered by Susan Au Allen), **Vital Speeches** v60 (September 1, 1994): p701.

Saint-Jean, Armande. "Rwanda," **Ms. Magazine** v5 (November-December 1994): p10.

Seymour, James D. "Human Rights in China," **Current History** v93 (September 1994): p256.

Silverstein, Ken. "Guerrillas in the Mist" (media misrepresentation of Rwanda), **Washington Monthly** v26 (September 1994): p21.

"Supporting Democracy" (Bill Clinton), **U.S. Department of State Dispatch** v5 (October 3, 1994): p649.

Urquidi, Mariclaire Acosta. "Human Rights, Official Torture, and the Future of Mexican Democracy," **Humanist** v54 (November-December 1994): p26.

Wirpsa, Leslie. "Haiti Becomes Laboratory for New U.S. Approach," **National Catholic Reporter** v30 (October 7, 1994): p7.

Wirpsa, Leslie. "140 Indigenous Leaders Killed Since 1990," **National Catholic Reporter** v31 (November 4, 1994): p14.